THE CANADA CAMPAIGN

1775–1776

Michael P. Gabriel

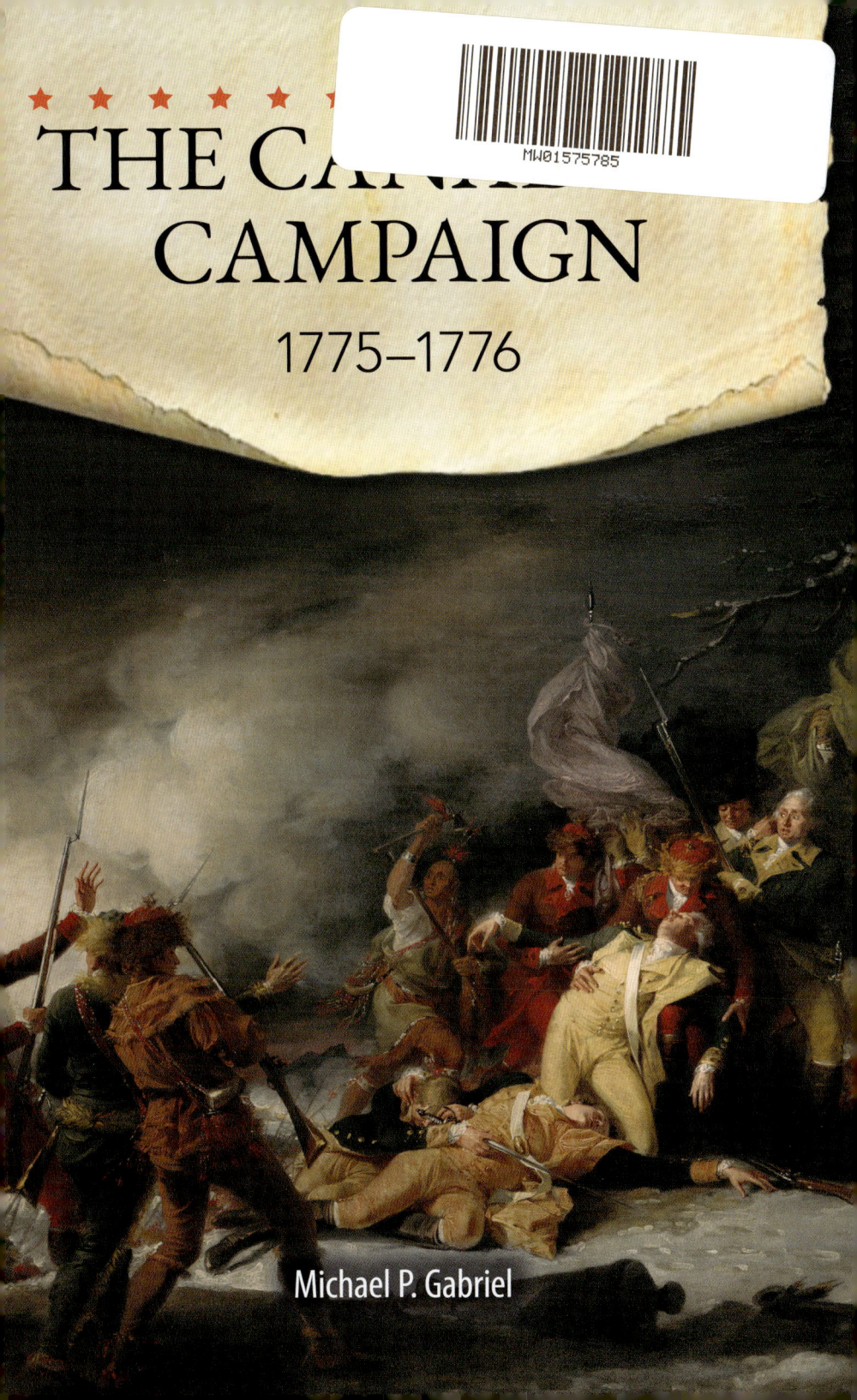

The U.S. Army Campaigns of the Revolutionary War

Series Editors
David W. Hogan Jr.
Joseph A. Seymour
Jonathan D. Bratten

Opening Shots in the Colonies, 1775–1776
The Canadian Campaign, 1775–1776
The New York Campaign, 1776
The New Jersey Campaign, 1776–1777
The Philadelphia Campaign, 1777
The Saratoga Campaign, 1777
Valley Forge to Monmouth, 1778
The War in the North, 1778–1781
The Frontier War, 1775–1783
The War in the South, 1778–1780
The War in the Carolinas and Georgia, 1781–1782
The War in Virginia, 1781
Securing Victory, 1781–1783

Cover: The Death of General Montgomery in the Attack on Quebec, December 31, 1775, John Trumbull, 1786 (*Yale University Art Gallery*)

The U.S. Army Campaigns of the Revolutionary War

THE CANADIAN CAMPAIGN
1775–1776

by
Michael P. Gabriel

Center of Military History
United States Army
Washington, D.C., 2024

Library of Congress Cataloging-in-Publication Data

Names: Gabriel, Michael P., 1962- author. | Center of Military History, issuing body.
Title: The Canadian campaign, 1775-1776 / by Michael P. Gabriel.
Other titles: U.S. Army campaigns of the Revolutionary War.
Description: Washington, D.C. : Center of Military History, United States Army, 2024.
Series: The U.S. Army campaigns of the Revolutionary War | In scope of the U.S. Government Publishing Office Cataloging and Indexing Program (C&I); not distributed in this format as part of the Federal Depository Library Program (FDLP). | Includes bibliographical references.
Identifiers: LCCN 2023048595 (print) | LCCN 2023048596 (ebook) | ISBN 9781959302087 (paperback) | ISBN 9781959302087 (Adobe pdf)
Subjects: LCSH: Canadian Invasion, 1775-1776. | United States--History--Revolution, 1775-1783--American forces.
Classification: LCC E231 .G33 2024 (print) | LCC E231 (ebook) | DDC 973.331--dc23/eng/20240130 | SUDOC D 114.7/9:C 16
LC record available at https://lccn.loc.gov/2023048595
LC ebook record available at https://lccn.loc.gov/2023048596

CMH Pub 71–43

 **CONTENTS**

Introduction 7

Strategic Setting 13

Operations 25

Conclusion and Analysis 83

Appendix 89

Bibliographic Note 95

The Author 97

Acknowledgment 97

Maps
1. American Invasion of Canada 12
2. Quebéc City 52

Note: We have retained the original spelling, capitalization, and punctuation in quoted materials.

INTRODUCTION

As America celebrates the 250th anniversary of the Revolutionary War, it is a perfect time to reflect on the revolutionary generation. In the two-and-a-half centuries since the war, the United States has grappled with the complexities and paradoxes of its revolution. How could a nation be born from the idea that all men are created equal, and yet deny much of that freedom to women and to many of its own population based on the color of their skin? How should a central federal government balance power with state governments? Could those thirteen fractious colonies merge into one nation? The seeds of what would become our country's future political and military conflicts lie in these complexities, as do some of our greatest national accomplishments.

This milestone anniversary is also an appropriate time to reflect on the history of the United States Army. The Army stands as our first truly national institution, having been established by the Continental Congress on 14 June 1775. General George Washington's ability to meld the soldiers of the various colonies together into one national force provided an example to the rest of the country that national unity was possible. If the Army failed to overcome the regional sectionalism prevalent at the time, it would fall to superior British resources and organization. If the Army failed, the nation would fail. Washington gave us the precedent of military subordination to the civil authority, one of the core tenets of our political tradition and way of life. At the end of the war, he resigned his commission and voluntarily gave up all his power to return to civil life. His example has inspired us as a model of military and political leadership for generations.

The Massachusetts militiamen who fired the first shots of the war on 19 April 1775 had no blueprint for creating a nation—nor did many think that the conflict would result in a drive for independence. Deep-seated colonial resentments over their rights as English citizens had been simmering since before the 1750s. As the British Parliament enacted even more restrictive laws, peaceful protests turned to military organization, and finally open violence. As New England formed its Army of Observation in the wake of the battles of Lexington and Concord, the Continental Congress saw the need for a national army.

For eight long years, the Continental Army maintained itself in the field, despite fighting superior odds, starvation, diminished resources, and divided leadership. Setbacks in the New York Campaign of 1776 nearly destroyed Washington's army as the British drove it into Pennsylvania. Yet as 1777 opened, Washington changed the operational situation by seizing the initiative in a series of tactical victories at Trenton and Princeton, New Jersey. That fall, a British invasion into northern New York met with failure and capture at the hands of the Northern Army and militia at Saratoga, ultimately bringing France into war on the side of the United States. At the same time, Washington kept a British army penned up in Philadelphia while he instituted a training regimen for his army at their encampment in Valley Forge that winter. Trained under the tutelage of German-born Frederick von Steuben, the Continentals harried the British out of Philadelphia and back to New York City, fighting like regulars at Monmouth in 1778.

General Washington faced the challenge of countering British victories at Charleston, South Carolina, and Savannah, Georgia, when the British shifted the war south in 1780, while also containing powerful British forces in Canada and New York City. Relying on skilled subordinates such as Anthony Wayne, Nathanael Greene, and the Marquis de Lafayette—all of whom in turn worked closely with state militia—Washington was able to hold the delicate balance of power in both the northern and southern theaters. Seizing the opportunity presented by his French allies, Washington quickly shifted a large portion of his army from New York City to Yorktown,

Virginia. There, the allies laid siege to another British army, forcing it to capitulate in the fall of 1781. Although this victory sounded the death knell for British control of the American colonies, peace talks would last for two more years. During this time, Washington kept an army in the field, maintained the supremacy of civil authority over the military, and presented a credible threat to the remaining British garrisons. When the peace came, the true architects of the revolution's success were the Continental Army, state troops, and the militia.

The Revolutionary War created the model for our modern Army. It set the stage for what eventually would become a three-component force, with the Continentals and militia operating in complementary roles. Today, thirty-three National Guard units can trace their lineage to the Revolutionary War, which is a testament to their role in the formation of this country. Eight army branches also have their beginnings in the revolution. The U.S. Army's very motto, "This We'll Defend," is rooted in the "self-evident" truths enunciated in the Declaration of Independence and American interpretations of Enlightenment traditions, which came together in the seal for the Board of War and Ordnance and became the Department of the Army seal in the twentieth century. Unfortunately, it also would take until the twentieth century for the U.S. Army to be as racially integrated as its Continental Army forebears.

The traditions begun and precedents set by Washington and his soldiers continue to influence the U.S. Army and causes around the world. The seeds of hope shown at Trenton and Princeton have inspired leaders in other dark times, such as Bull Run, Shiloh, and Kasserine Pass. The revolutionary generation taught us that the true strength of our Army is our people; from the frontline soldiers to the camp followers who sustained the regiments. And it is to these individuals, who forged ahead through privation and misery to final victory and who rarely received any greater recognition in their own lifetimes than the simple epitaph "A Soldier of the Revolution," that these volumes are humbly dedicated.

CHARLES R. BOWERY JR.
Executive Director

THE CANADIAN CAMPAIGN 1775–1776

In the months following the opening shots at Lexington and Concord on 19 April 1775, Americans seized the initiative and took the fight to the British. Near Boston, 20,000 militiamen, known as the New England Army of Observation, laid siege to the city. Meanwhile, the growing American rebellion spread from Massachusetts to the Champlain Valley in New York and present-day Vermont. On 10 May, Ethan Allen and some of his Green Mountain Boys captured Fort Ticonderoga in New York and its large store of artillery and other military equipment. Accompanying Allen was Benedict Arnold, a Connecticut militia officer whom the Massachusetts Committee of Safety commissioned to attack the fort. Simultaneously, another group of Green Mountain Boys occupied nearby Skenesborough and seized a schooner belonging to the settlement's loyalist founder, Philip W. Skene. The next day, Allen's associate, Seth Warner, captured a second British installation at nearby Crown Point along with additional military stores. Arnold subsequently sailed north in Skene's vessel, which he renamed the *Liberty*, and raided a third fortification, Saint-Jean, Québec, on

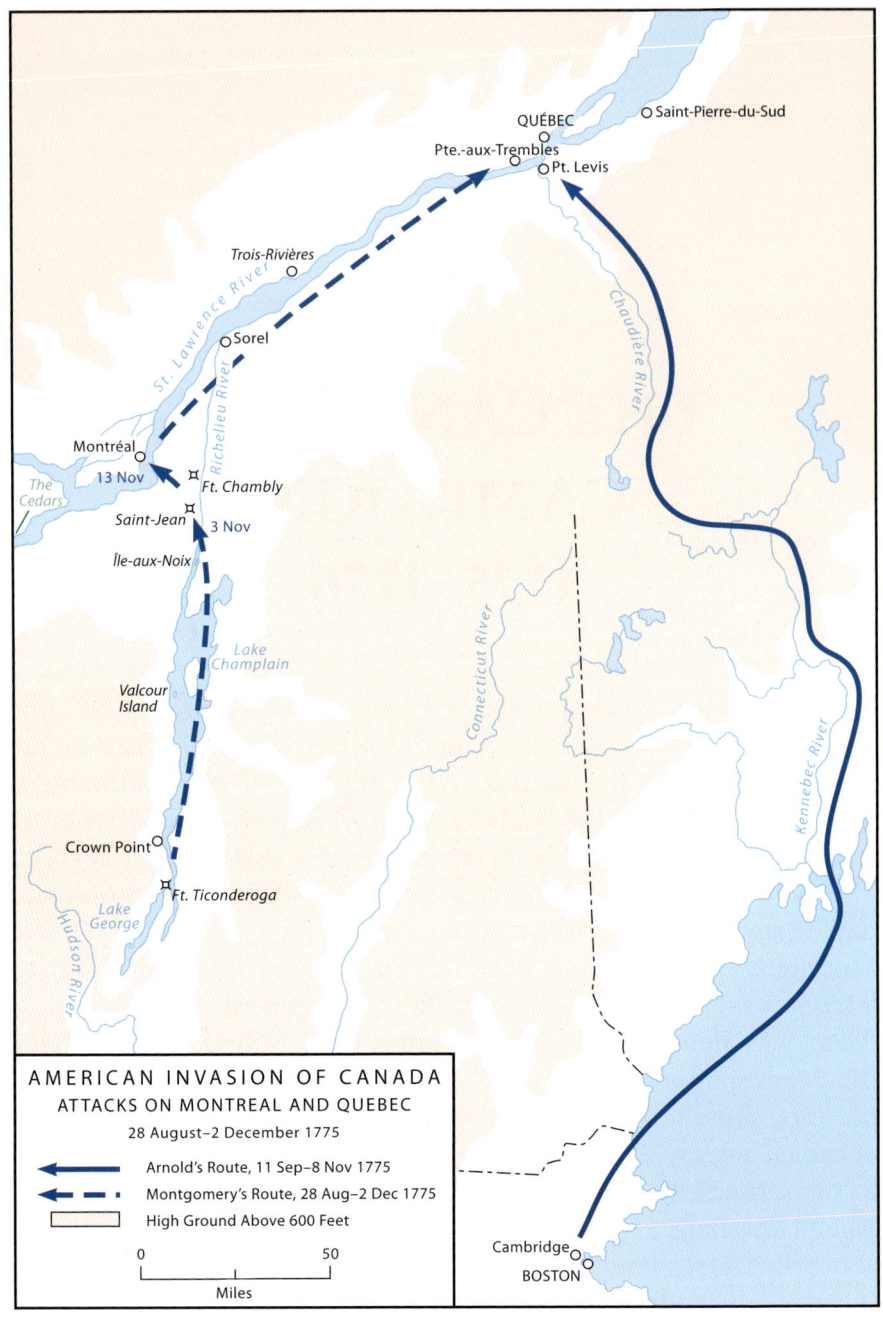

Map 1

the Richelieu River approximately 25 miles southeast of Montréal on 18 May. Arnold captured the fort's small garrison of thirteen, two brass 6-pounder cannons, and a British sloop, later dubbed the *Enterprise*, before retiring to Ticonderoga. He also seized a letter from Québec's governor, Maj. Gen. Guy Carleton, stating that he possessed fewer than 700 regulars to defend the colony. Although the Second Continental Congress (which had not even met until the day Ticonderoga fell) did not authorize or approve these operations, they had far-reaching consequences. Allen and Arnold had given the Americans undisputed control of Lake Champlain and opened the door for American forces to invade Canada (*Map 1*).

 STRATEGIC SETTING

Canadian Context

In 1775, Great Britain ruled four colonies that are now part of present-day Canada—Québec, Nova Scotia, Newfoundland, and St. John's Island (present-day Prince Edward Island). When the First Continental Congress met in Philadelphia in fall 1774, it had invited Québec to send delegates, believing it also faced tyranny under British rule. Québec had only come under British control in 1763 because of France's defeat in the Seven Years' War. The former French colony had some grievances in common with its counterparts to the south, but its situation was also different in significant ways.

The majority of the 110,000 people who resided in Québec were French-speaking tenant farmers—*habitants*—who lived in small communities that lined the St. Lawrence River. It was a semifeudal

General Sir Guy Carleton, Mabel B. Messer, 1923 (*Library and Archives Canada*)

system, with the habitants renting from and owing obligations and fees to large landowners known as *seigneurs*. The habitants had grown more prosperous under the economic stability that the British created after taking control of the colony from France in 1763. The British also had reduced the privileges of the seigneurs and some of the payments the habitants had owed under the old system. Still, the attachment of these former French colonists—so-called New Subjects of the British Crown—to Britain remained questionable, having to overcome generations of hatred from four bitter wars against Britain and its American colonists. In addition to the French Canadians, several thousand British and Americans—Old Subjects—settled in Québec after 1763, most of them merchants and traders attracted by the fur trade and other economic opportunities. They mainly resided near Montréal, Québec City, and Trois-Rivières, the colony's three main settlements.

Britain initially ruled Québec by a royal edict, but its first two governors, James Murray and Guy Carleton, recognized the need for a government more in keeping with its traditional French regime. Parliament's passage of the Quebec Act in June 1774 represented an attempt to meet this need and assimilate the French Canadians into the British Empire. The act's main provisions expanded Québec's boundaries to include the lands west of the Appalachian Mountains and north of the Ohio River—today, the states of Ohio, Michigan, Indiana, Illinois, Wisconsin, and parts of Minnesota—and provided for the use of French civil law while retaining British criminal law. The Quebec Act also created an appointed council, recognized the legitimacy of the Roman Catholic Church in the colony, and allowed Catholics to participate in governance by eliminating the Oath of Supremacy to the British sovereign as the head of the Church of England.

Despite its good intentions, the Quebec Act did not receive universal acclaim. Many of the recent British and American arrivals objected that the act lacked traditional British political rights, most notably an elective assembly, even though they had requested one since 1763. Consequently, sporadic protests occurred, most notably in Montréal, and calls for the act's repeal appeared. The French Canadian habitants also did not necessarily welcome the Quebec Act, despite Parliament's efforts to draft a piece of legislation that reflected their established traditions. It clearly favored the seigneurs by granting them political rights and potentially restoring their feudal privileges over the habitants. The habitants were also suspicious of British criminal law. One British loyalist commented that "the

Canadian Peasants began to shew a disposition little to be expected from a conquer'd people who had been treated with so much lenity by Government." He further noted that the habitants were influenced partly by "the never ceasing labours of the Malcontents in this Province," who clamored against the Quebec Act.

The American colonists strongly disliked the Quebec Act, which they considered a part of the Intolerable Acts that Parliament had imposed on them at approximately the same time. They saw it as further evidence of the conspiracy against liberty and an ominous portent of the future. Americans further believed that the act's assignment of territory to Québec, along with the Royal Proclamation of 1763 that prohibited settlement in Indian territory, deprived them of access to the rich lands beyond the Appalachians. They also feared the precedent of the establishment of an arbitrary government based on an appointed council with no elective assembly. Finally, the colonists, especially New Englanders who had fought repeated wars against the Catholic French of Québec, felt betrayed by the act's tolerance of a religion that they associated with absolutism and England's historic enemies, France and Spain. If Parliament possessed the power to pass such an act for Québec, could it do the same for the American colonies? Parliament seemed to have designed the Quebec Act to establish tyranny, appease the French Canadians, and create a staging area from which Britain could threaten the New York and New England frontier.

Geography enhanced this potential menace, as the strategic St. Lawrence River–Lake Champlain–Hudson River corridor historically had provided invading armies with an avenue to move north and south. Whoever controlled Lake Champlain possessed a great strategic advantage. Stretching 107 miles, the lake flowed into the Richelieu River, which entered the St. Lawrence River below Montréal. This entire route was navigable except for a stretch of the Richelieu blocked by the Chambly Rapids. Saint-Jean stood on the western bank of the river at the southern end of the rapids. Fort Chambly was situated on the same shore at the northern terminus of the rapids. Île-aux-Noix, a low swampy island 12 miles south of Saint-Jean, offered the only other obstacle to shipping on the Champlain-Richelieu water route. From this island in the Richelieu, a defender could block access into or out of Lake Champlain. Despite its strategic location, the British left Île-aux-Noix unoccupied. Thick primeval forests, interspersed with large swamps, lined this corridor, making overland passage nearly impossible.

The St. Lawrence flowed east from the Great Lakes to the Atlantic Ocean, and it connected Canada's three main settlements, Montréal, Trois-Rivières, and Québec. Sailing west against the current was possible, but it became increasingly dangerous because of islands and rapids near Montréal. The Chemin du Roy, a road on the north bank of the river, also connected the three population centers but was less reliable, except in winter when Canada's heavy snow allowed for the use of sleds. These proved advantageous because the St. Lawrence frequently froze from late fall until spring, isolating the colony from Britain.

Lake Champlain did not connect to the Hudson River, which flowed south past Albany and into the Atlantic at New York City. Two routes, both of which Native Americans used for centuries, bridged the gap of about 25 miles. The first ran south from Lake George 16 miles overland to Fort Edward, New York, on the Hudson. The other ran from Skenesborough, on the southern tip of Lake Champlain, to Fort Edward by way of Wood Creek. This latter route became more heavily used after 1775 as the Canadian Campaign progressed.

British Crown Forces

Carleton, the royal governor, also commanded British forces in Québec. Born into a Protestant British family in Ireland, he had entered the army in 1742 and saw extensive service during the Seven Years' War in Europe, the Caribbean, and North America—including at Louisbourg, Nova Scotia, and Québec City. He served first as lieutenant-governor of Québec and then took on the duties of governor in 1768. As governor, Carlton was committed deeply to the Canadian people, and he largely developed the Quebec Act and lobbied for its passage. Reserved, level-headed, and staunchly loyal to the British Crown, he possessed sound judgement and favored leniency and reconciliation with the Americans.

In the spring of 1775, Carleton relied on a collection of British regulars, militia, and Native Americans to defend Canada and help suppress rebellion to the south. The preceding September, British General Thomas Gage requested that Carleton send him reinforcements in Boston to meet the growing crisis there. Carleton dispatched the *10th* and *52d Regiments of Foot*, partly based on the belief that militia could help meet Québec's military needs. This left three regiments of British regulars in Canada. One of these, the *8th Regiment of Foot*, occupied various outposts in the Great Lakes, such as Fort Niagara, New York, and Michilimackinac Island in present-day Michigan. This left only the *7th* and *26th Regiments of Foot* to garrison the St. Lawrence Valley. Reductions in the size of the British Army following the Seven Years' War and recruitment problems left both regiments understrength, totaling around 700 soldiers, most of whom Carleton deployed near Montréal. Lt. Col. Allan Maclean also was recruiting a provincial regiment, the *Royal Highland Emigrants*, among Scottish settlers in Canada and the northern colonies. By August 1775, he could field 500 recruits. Many of the officers and enlisted men in these regiments possessed prior military experience, but relatively few of them were available to defend the sprawling colony.

Potentially, Carleton also could have drawn upon both British and French Canadian militia, but their numbers and effectiveness were much in doubt. On 9 June, responding to the situation in Massachusetts and Arnold's raid on Saint-Jean, the governor declared martial law in Canada and called out the militia, "so treasonable invasion may be soon defeated, and all traitors with their...abetters, may be speedily brought to justice." Many of the Old Subjects resented the Quebec Act, however, and they demonstrated little enthusiasm to serve. For example, in Québec City only seventy merchants and citizens attended a mid-July meeting to organize the "British Militia," and a similar situation existed in Montréal. In general, most Old Subjects might have turned out only if the Americans directly threatened their lives and property, but Carleton could not count on them to participate in offensive actions.

The situation was even worse among the French Canadians. Carleton, not surprisingly, depended upon the seigneurs to rally their tenants for militia service, but this initiative had disastrous results. In several communities near Montréal and in the Richelieu River Valley, the habitants resisted calls to enlist. The most extreme case occurred near Chambly, where the locals thrashed their seigneur's son when he haughtily demanded their service. As many as 3,000 habitants then armed themselves with farm implements and weapons upon hearing rumors that British regulars were marching against them. They did not disperse until Carleton sent word that he would not send troops. Similar events occurred near Québec City. Habitants held a "seditious rally" at Pointe-Lévy at which they invited nearby settlements to resist British efforts, and fourteen communities posted guards to protect themselves from troops.

Carleton also potentially could have employed Native Americans for Canada's defense, including the Six Nations of the Iroquois Confederacy (Haudenosaunee) and the Seven Nations of Canada. The latter groups consisted of tribes residing in the St. Lawrence Valley, including the Kahnawake (a branch of the Mohawks who had settled near Montréal), the Abenaki, and the Hurons. To assist him in this, he could call on Maj. John Campbell, the superintendent of Indian affairs for Québec, and Daniel Claus and Guy Johnson, royal Indian agents, who had fled from New York to Canada that spring. In July 1775, Johnson and Claus held a conference in Montréal with 1,600 Iroquois and members of the Seven Nations and enlisted their support of the British cause. Carleton, however, did not want to employ them in offensive actions against the colonists, even though he had received permission to do so from William Legge, 2nd Earl of Dartmouth, the British Secretary of State for the Colonies. Carleton believed that working alongside Native Americans might further alienate the Americans and hurt the chances of reconciliation

Richard Montgomery, Charles Willson Peale, 1784–1786 *(Independence National Historical Park)*

with Britain. He also thought that their style of irregular warfare represented a two-edged sword. Although useful for reconnaissance, skirmishing, and intimidating opponents, it created command-and-control issues. Instead, with Johnson's assistance, Carleton rotated groups of forty to fifty Abenaki to the Saint-Jean area to help guard the colony's border.

A number of fortifications bolstered Canada's defenses. Still, the same budget cuts that had reduced the army's size left many of these—including Saint-Jean, Ticonderoga, and Crown Point—

in disrepair at the time of the American raids in May. Carleton immediately began to strengthen these outposts and had made great progress by the time the Americans invaded.

American Forces

Following Allen and Arnold's seizure of Ticonderoga, the patriot forces in New York attempted to garrison the fort but lacked the resources to do so adequately. The Second Continental Congress assumed this responsibility in late May by ordering Col. Benjamin Hinman's 4th Connecticut Regiment to hold the fort and by authorizing New York to raise 3,000 soldiers at Continental expense to guard its territory. Congressional influence grew with the creation of the Continental Army on 14 June 1775, when it adopted the troops near Boston and in New York and appointed George Washington as its commanding general the following day. Several days later, Congress commissioned Philip J. Schuyler as a major general and placed him in command of the New York or Northern Department (a geographic or theater command in today's parlance), with Brig. Gen. Richard Montgomery as his second-in-command.

Schuyler, a member of an old, elite New York family, was short on combat experience but possessed strong logistical skills. During the Seven Years' War, he had served with Col. John Bradstreet while supplying Fort Oswego, New York, and provisioned Maj. Gen. Jeffery Amherst's army during its 1759–1760 campaigns against Ticonderoga and Montréal. Schuyler's extensive business connections, coupled with his ties to the Albany Committee of Safety and the New York Provincial Congress, further enhanced his logistical efforts.

Montgomery, a former British Army captain in the 17th Regiment of Foot, served on Lake Champlain and in the Caribbean during the Seven Years' War and later in Pontiac's Uprising. He settled in New York in 1772 and subsequently married Janet Livingston, which brought him into the influential Livingston family. A reluctant delegate to the New York Provincial Congress,

Montgomery similarly accepted a brigadier general's commission in the Continental Army. Although he was hesitant to give up his private life to fight the British, he strongly believed in the American cause. Personally brave and used to leading from the front, Montgomery possessed the combat experience Schuyler lacked and earned his troops' devotion.

Over the summer, Schuyler's command—sometimes referred to as the "Separate Army" to distinguish it from Washington's command near Boston—continued to grow. In addition to Hinman's and four New York regiments, it also included Col. David Wooster's and Col. David Waterbury's 1st and 5th Connecticut Regiments, which Congress ordered north from New York City. Congress also assigned a detachment of Massachusetts soldiers under Col. James Easton to the Northern Department, as well as Capt. John Lamb's New York artillery company.

These units, the core of the fledgling Continental Army in the north, had little uniformity in organization and training. Their varied internal dynamics also reflected the differences in the colonies that raised them. Created on 1 May, the Connecticut regiments each consisted of 10 companies and numbered a total of approximately 1,100 soldiers. They also previously had served in New York City and New England before marching north. Throughout the campaign, Schuyler and Montgomery, both New Yorkers, complained about what they regarded as the overly democratic nature of New England troops and the equality that existed between the officers and enlisted men. New York, by contrast, did not begin to raise its regiments until late June; although these units also included 10 companies, they totaled only 750 troops. The New York regiments, which lacked the same equality between officers and soldiers, reflected the colony's stratified society. Still, by November, Montgomery commented that "the sweepings of New York's streets" who composed the 1st New York Regiment seemed "more like Regular troops, than I have seen in the Continental service." The enlistments of the troops from both colonies, however, expired in late 1775, causing major problems later in the campaign.

The newly created Green Mountain Boys, also from Schuyler's command, similarly reflected the differences and tensions among the colonists. Both New York and New Hampshire claimed the Hampshire Grants—present-day Vermont—but most of its residents received their land from the latter colony. Ethan Allen therefore formed the Green Mountain Boys in the years before the war to protect these claims from New York. On 23 June 1775, Congress authorized a Green Mountain unit in recognition of Allen's role in capturing Ticonderoga and his militia's wilderness combat skills. Given the unit's history as a formerly antagonistic force, New York did not want the Green Mountain Boys included as one of its units, so Schuyler raised it under Congress. Totaling 500 divided into 7 companies, the regiment elected reliable Seth Warner as its colonel, rather than the loud, ambitious Allen.

By August, Schuyler had 1,847 soldiers stationed at Ticonderoga and nearby Forts Edward and George on the Hudson River and Lake George. This number continued to grow, but units often arrived incomplete. An organized order of battle remains difficult to determine. Still, by 15 November 1775, the following units served with the Northern Army: the 1st, 2d, 3d, and 4th New York Regiments; the 1st, 4th, and 5th Connecticut; Easton's Massachusetts Regiment; Col. Timothy Bedel's New Hampshire Rangers; the Green Mountain Boys; James Livingston's 1st Canadian Regiment; Edward Mott's company of the 6th Connecticut Regiment; John Lamb's New York Artillery; and Montgomery's provisional artillery section. Ticonderoga remained the main staging area for American troops during the rest of the Canadian Campaign, through its conclusion in November 1776. Soldiers from six different colonies and Canada ultimately passed through the fort on their way north and south.

Some African American soldiers served in the Northern Army, but the exact number remains unknown. Each colony had its own regulations concerning Black participation in the militia, with some fearing that this would undermine slavery or even lead to slave revolts. The New England colonies, which had relatively small Black populations compared to colonies farther south, allowed African

Americans to serve from the beginning of the Revolutionary War. Some of those who served were free, others joined the military to obtain their freedom, and others never received it. Still, New England African Americans had fought at Lexington, Concord, and Bunker Hill, and continued to do so throughout the entire Canadian Campaign. Cash Affrica, from Litchfield, served at Saint-Jean in Wooster's 1st Connecticut, as did London Dow, Prime Wheeler, Stephen Lovewell, and John Freeman in Bedel's New Hampshire Rangers.

Native Americans, especially the Six Nations of the Iroquois, figured prominently in American planning during the Canadian Campaign. At this point in the revolution, Congress did not seek support actively from the Iroquois or other Native American groups and instead hoped to convince them to remain neutral. In late August, Schuyler and other American delegates met with the Iroquois tribes—mainly Oneida, Tuscarora, and Mohawk—in Albany on Congress's behalf. Schuyler's social and military status served him well, as did the fact that the Mohawk respected him as the grandnephew of Peter Schuyler, Albany's first mayor, who had been their faithful friend. The American delegates argued that the current conflict between the king and the colonists did not involve the Native Americans and that they should stay neutral. The commissioners also referred several Iroquois grievances and requests to Congress and presented them with gifts. The Iroquois accepted the calls for neutrality and expressed the hope that neither side would interfere with their trade, at which point the conference adjourned. Schuyler had achieved Congress's goal, at least for the time being.

 # OPERATIONS

Initial Planning and Coordination

The news of Allen and Arnold's seizure of Fort Ticonderoga created a dilemma for the Second Continental Congress. Some delegates welcomed the act, but moderates expressed concern that this unauthorized offensive action might hinder a political settlement with Britain. Congress ultimately adopted a middle position by endorsing the attack on the grounds of self-defense, claiming that indisputable evidence proved the British were preparing to attack the New York and New England frontier. Still, Congress considered returning Ticonderoga and Crown Point to the British and ordered the forts' garrisons to inventory their military supplies and move them to a secure location. The Americans would then return them to Britain with the restoration of peace. Although it eventually reversed this decision, Congress's vacillation demonstrated its uncertainty over what to do with the forts—and, ultimately, with Canada.

This debate over the next step continued throughout May and June. Congress sent additional letters in both French and English to their "Friends and Countrymen" to the north, justifying the colonists' actions and claiming that they were fighting for the rights of Canadians as well. However, some Americans, especially those from New York and New England, wanted more aggressive actions. A strongly fortified American-held Ticonderoga would shield the frontier from British attacks like those the French had launched during the colonial wars. Furthermore, both Arnold and Allen suggested that American forces preemptively seize lightly defended Montréal to remove permanently the threat to the northern frontier and demonstrate American resolve to the British government. It would also deprive the British of a rich source of grain and expand the rebellion's base of support.

A steady stream of intelligence from Canada influenced this debate and gradually changed Congress's sentiments. Some reports claimed that the Canadians would welcome an American incursion and might even send delegates to Philadelphia. More importantly, other reports suggested that Carleton was preparing to attack. He had deployed troops to Saint-Jean, was building warships there, and was encouraging the Native Americans to strike the American frontier. Although this last piece of intelligence was inaccurate, it spurred Congress to act. In the face of this growing threat, on 27 June, Congress ordered Schuyler to "take possession of St. Johns [Saint-Jean], Montreal, and any other parts of the country" if "it will not be disagreeable to the Canadians."

Although Congress now had authorized an invasion, Schuyler needed time to organize his forces. Similar to the problems Washington faced near Boston, a chronic shortage of nearly everything hindered Schuyler's efforts. Lack of wagons and shipping slowed the army's march, as did the poor roads between Albany and Ticonderoga. When the soldiers arrived, they frequently needed such basic items as shoes, blankets, tents, kettles, muskets, and bayonets. The Americans were also short of gunpowder, and they remained so throughout much of the campaign. Schuyler received 2,750 pounds of gunpowder in July, but this did not meet the great demand.

Furthermore, intercolonial rivalries existed among the soldiers from New England and New York, with both groups commenting negatively on each other. Connecticut officers noted how few New York troops actually had arrived at Ticonderoga by August and suggested that the colony lacked a commitment for "So Just a Cause." New Yorkers responded by disparaging their eastern neighbors' unruliness and lack of order. Amid these difficulties, illness broke out among the troops. Many of the soldiers came from isolated farms and small villages and had never been exposed to large numbers of people and the diseases they carried. The soldiers also lacked basic knowledge about hygiene and camp discipline.

Schuyler and Montgomery worked diligently to address these problems. Both tried to instill discipline among the inexperienced soldiers and train them in the ways of war. Moreover, Schuyler drew on his many connections to obtain provisions, and he implemented an ambitious program to build large, flat-bottomed boats—known as *bateaux*—and other vessels, along with barrels, to aid in transporting troops and provisions. Montgomery tried to get birch bark so his troops could brew medicinal beer to combat camp fevers and other maladies, and he established a military hospital in Albany. Still, disease remained a major problem and Schuyler himself fell sick. By 6 August, nearly 20 percent of the troops at Ticonderoga were too ill for military duty; between 20 July and 25 September, Schuyler discharged 726 unhealthy soldiers. The American preparations continued despite these problems.

As Schuyler and Montgomery prepared their forces on Lake Champlain for an attack on Saint-Jean and Montréal, George Washington considered a second operation against Canada. As early as the 1680s, French military officials in Québec City had suggested attacking New England by sending troops through the Maine wilderness by way of the Chaudière and Kennebec Rivers. The British considered using this same route, albeit in the opposite direction, during the Seven Years' War. In 1761, Capt. John Montresor of the Royal Engineers demonstrated the route's existence when he and a small party traveled and mapped the Chaudière-Kennebec corridor to Maine. Thoughts of attacking Québec City through the Maine wilderness resurfaced after fighting broke out at Lexington and Concord, and Washington obtained a copy of Montresor's map when he took command of the army at Cambridge. Washington gained further intelligence about this route from residents who lived on the Kennebec and a Native American chief who had traveled along it. Washington probably discussed the idea with Benedict Arnold when the two first met on 10 August. Through these meetings Washington came to believe that a small, lightly armed force could complete this expedition successfully in approximately three weeks.

On 20 August, Washington informed Schuyler about the proposed expedition against Québec City, explaining that it would help the Montréal attack by forcing Carleton to divide his forces. "He

Col. Benedict Arnold with Québec in the background (*Library of Congress*)

must either break up and follow this Party to Québeck, by which he will leave you a free Passage, or he must suffer that important Place to fall into our Hands." Unfortunately for the American cause, the Montresor map lacked key details on parts of the route and did not reflect fully the wilderness's rugged terrain.

Montgomery's Advance to Montréal

Before Washington finished planning the Maine expedition, the American army on Lake Champlain invaded Canada. On 25 August, with Schuyler in Albany for the Indian conference, Montgomery received urgent intelligence that two British warships under construction at Saint-Jean would be ready to sail within ten days. If this occurred, the British would gain naval control on the lake, thwarting an American attack. Therefore, Montgomery decided to act. As he wrote to Schuyler, "The moving without your orders I don't like, but on the other hand, the prevention of the enemy is of the utmost consequence. If I must err I wish to be on the right side."

Despite the urgency of the situation, Montgomery took three days to assemble a force of nearly 1,200 soldiers, composed of Waterbury's 5th Connecticut Regiment, a company of Connecticut artillery, and four companies of the 1st New York Regiment. A motley fleet consisting of the *Liberty*, the *Enterprise*, two large flat-bottomed gunboats—the *Schuyler* and the *Hancock*, each mounted with one 12-pounder cannon—and numerous bateaux and whaleboats sailed at 1800 on 28 August. The troops had high morale and a great commitment to the American cause. One soldier wrote, "Your countrymen with united voices cry aloud for your utmost exercion in this time of need . . . pray to arms, to arms my friends! . . . I had rather never again return from the field, than live and die a slave."

The American Army sailed north on Lake Champlain, but "a Barbarous north wind" delayed their progress. It did not arrive at Isle la Motte, approximately 25 miles south of Saint-Jean, until 1 September. Schuyler joined the army three days later. It then immediately advanced to Île-aux-Noix where Schuyler issued a proclamation to the Canadians and local tribes, saying that the Americans came as liberators. He also noted that they had made peace with the Iroquois and had presents for the Kahnawake. This message demonstrated that diplomatic considerations carried nearly as much importance as military ones. Without Canadian and Indian support, or at least neutrality, the invasion could not succeed, and throughout the campaign American commanders cautioned their troops not to alienate civilians by looting and other acts.

Schuyler, who remained ill, made two attempts to isolate Saint-Jean, but both failed, partly because of the soldiers' inexperience. On 6 September, Montgomery landed south of the British force with 1,000 troops, and then skirmished with 100 Native Americans and Canadian loyalists. With the afternoon nearly gone and the green soldiers disorganized by the fighting, the Americans returned to the landing site. They subsequently withdrew another mile farther south when they came under British artillery fire from the fort. That night, Schuyler received intelligence that Carleton had fortified Saint-Jean heavily and deployed most of the British *26th Regiment of Foot* nearby, along with approximately one hundred Native Americans. Furthermore, although the local inhabitants favored the Americans, they would not support them actively until assured of their success. Finally, Schuyler learned that the *Royal Savage*, a sixteen-gun schooner, was nearly ready to sail. Believing that he lacked the necessary artillery to lay siege to the fort or sink the *Royal Savage*, Schuyler returned to Île-aux-Noix. There he prepared to build a boom across the river to prevent the schooner from passing into Lake Champlain and waited for reinforcements and word from the Canadians.

On 8 September, reinforcements arrived at Île-aux-Noix, bringing the American strength to 1,700 soldiers supported by 5 cannons and 2 mortars. That same day, Schuyler received a letter from James Livingston, a cousin of Montgomery's wife and a local resident, saying that Schuyler's proclamation had encouraged the Canadians greatly. Livingston claimed that he and a large group of habitants would meet the army when it returned to Saint-Jean. To capture the fort, he recommended that Schuyler immediately isolate the garrison by cutting the roads to Chambly and Montréal. This seemed like sound advice to the major general, and he issued orders to implement it.

Two days later, Schuyler made his second attempt to besiege Saint-Jean. Montgomery and 800 soldiers landed 3 miles south of the fort around 2030, and twice began marching north to block the roads to Montréal and Chambly. Both times, however, they became confused in the dark, swampy forest and returned to the landing site. The following morning, before Montgomery could make a third attempt, a scout erroneously reported the *Royal Savage*'s approach. Knowing that his flotilla lacked the firepower to take on the schooner, Montgomery reluctantly ordered the entire force back to Île-aux-Noix.

Over the next two days, rainy weather, a lack of provisions, and the general realization of the difficulties facing them sapped the soldiers' health and spirits. By 12 September, at least 600 soldiers had fallen ill, and discipline problems suggested low morale.

Still, some cause for optimism existed. Schuyler received several intelligence reports, including additional letters from Livingston. The reports indicated that the Canadians saw the Americans as friends, and Livingston had assembled 300 habitants and could raise 3,000 when the army appeared. Additionally, he had attacked a small British detachment, taken two prisoners, and planned to send the Americans fifty-nine loaves of bread and sixteen quarters of beef. Reinforcements also continued to arrive at Île-aux-Noix, including a company of New York troops, a Green Mountain Boys detachment, Capt. John Lamb's New York artillery company, and part of Col. Timothy Bedel's three companies of New Hampshire Rangers.

Based on these developments, Schuyler decided to make a third attempt at Saint-Jean. On 13 September, he issued orders for the Northern Army to resume the advance in two days and, on the 14th, sent one hundred Americans and thirty-four Canadians to Chambly to maintain the habitants' morale. Heavy rains delayed the army's departure, and on 16 September, Schuyler's health collapsed. He could no longer serve in the field and returned to Ticonderoga, leaving Montgomery in command. Schuyler continued to contribute to the American cause by sending a steady stream of soldiers and provisions to Canada. The next day, Montgomery and approximately 1,400 soldiers landed several miles south of the fort and their gunboats exchanged several ineffectual volleys with the British garrison.

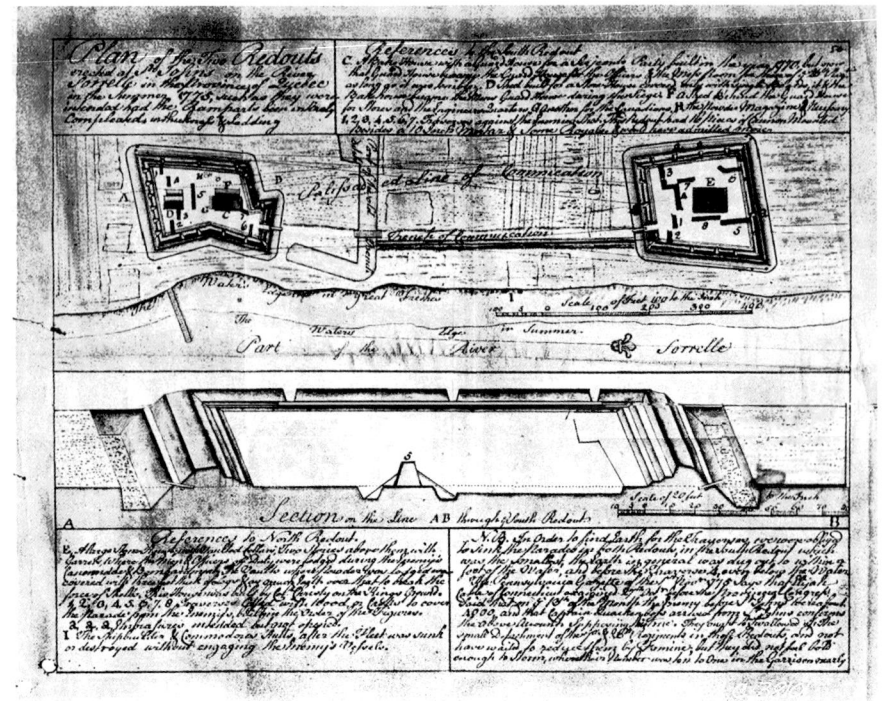

A plan of Fort St. John (*Library and Archives Canada*)

Maj. Charles Preston of the *26th Regiment of Foot* commanded Saint-Jean, two sodded earthen redoubts about 600 feet apart, surrounded by a deep trench reinforced with *fraises* (stakes driven into the ground with the pointed end facing out). The southern redoubt contained a number of buildings, including a powder magazine, whereas the northern one enclosed a large, two-story stone house, which served as a barracks. The garrison had cleared the forest and brush for several hundred yards around the redoubts to create fields of fire. Saint-Jean's garrison consisted of 239 soldiers from the *7th Regiment of Foot*, 198 from the 26th, 18 *Royal Highland Emigrants*, 31 *Royal Artillerymen*, and 71 volunteers, mainly Canadian seigneurs, for a total of 557. Ten sailors manned the *Royal Savage*, which lay at anchor between the two redoubts, as did a nearly finished row galley. Approximately eighty women and children also took shelter in the fort. Preston

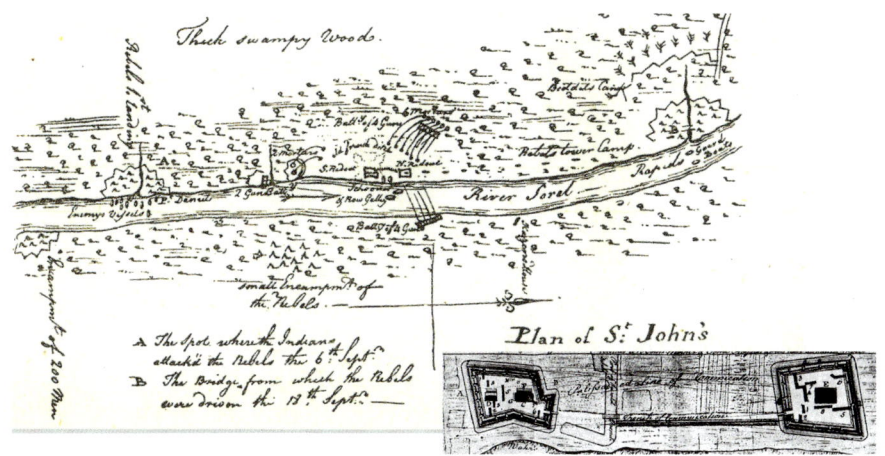

The siege of Fort St. John (*Library and Archives Canada*)

had adequate ammunition and military equipment, including forty artillery pieces, but he lacked food for an extended siege.

That evening, the soldiers that Schuyler had sent into Canada several days earlier, opened the action north of the fort. They cut the road between Saint-Jean and La Prairie, a crossing point to Montréal on the St. Lawrence, by destroying a bridge and intercepting eight supply carts heading to the garrison. The following morning, two hundred British and Canadians counterattacked but failed to reopen the road and recover the provisions.

Over the next several days, the Americans finished encircling Saint-Jean. Bedel's Rangers established the main camp north of the fort, while other detachments guarded La Prairie and Longueuil, a village on the St. Lawrence, to prevent any British crossings from Montréal. Still other soldiers watched Chambly, while Ethan Allen, who served as a volunteer with the army, attempted to recruit Canadians. Four hundred other soldiers established a fortified camp south of Saint-Jean, while Montgomery placed six vessels across the Richelieu to fend off the *Royal Savage*. This deployment effectively isolated the British fort from relief, but it stretched the American troops to the limit.

The Americans began formal siege operations by building *fascines*—bundles of wood they used like sandbags—and a road for the artillery. They completed the road by 22 September and then began to erect a mortar battery 600 yards south of Saint-Jean, but they encountered difficulties. Heavy, persistent rains flooded the already swampy lowlands along the Richelieu. This rain slowed the construction of siege works, limited the bombardment of the fort, and interfered with the movement of troops and supplies. Montgomery described the Northern Army as "half-drowned rats crawling thro' the Swamps." The army also lacked necessary provisions such as pork, rum, and flour. The high price of food in Canada, especially flour, exacerbated these shortages, and on 24 September, Montgomery placed his troops on half rations. These accumulated factors led to the continued outbreak of illness, which further weakened the army. Montgomery sent the sick to Île-aux-Noix or even Ticonderoga because he lacked adequate hospital facilities. By 12 October, Schuyler had discharged 937 soldiers because of illness. The soldiers who remained at Saint-Jean also suffered from a shortage of gunpowder and artillery shells, and the army's cannons and mortars lacked the weight to batter the fort into submission. Montgomery repeatedly asked Schuyler for additional troops, ordnance, artillery, and provisions, and by the end of the September he questioned if the army possessed the strength to take Saint-Jean.

These difficulties lowered the morale of the green American troops. Desertions began to rise, along with illness, and others grumbled about the harsh conditions, hard work, and lack of food. The officers were not immune to these complaints, and some lacked commitment to the cause. Most disheartening, Ethan Allen suffered a humiliating defeat at Montréal while recruiting near Chambly.

Allen and several officers who commanded detachments north of Saint-Jean had discussed the possibility of attacking Montréal, which lay on an island in the St. Lawrence. They had received intelligence that the city's defenses were in disrepair and that a large number of residents would support an American attack. Capturing Montréal would doom Forts Saint-Jean and Chambly, enhance American prestige, and secure valuable provisions. After meeting with several pro-American residents and without informing the other officers, Allen decided to attack Montréal on 25 September with around eighty soldiers, about two-thirds of whom were Canadians. Instead of being welcomed by residents, however, Allen found himself attacked by 34 regulars and 200 pro-British volunteers. His troops scattered after 20 minutes, leaving five dead and thirty-three captured, including Allen. British losses at what became known as the Battle of Longue-Pointe included one killed and three wounded. Allen's defeat gave the Canadians pause in supporting the Americans and briefly revived Carleton's recruiting efforts.

Despite these problems and setbacks, the American situation gradually improved. The heavy rains temporarily ceased, although the weather remained cold and wet. Equally important, Schuyler redoubled his efforts to provision the Northern Army in the face of the general shortages that plagued the Americans throughout the Revolutionary War. To overcome a persistent lack of boats and barrels, he ordered Montgomery to return both after his troops unloaded them. Montgomery complied by sending empty barrels back to Ticonderoga on boats manned by "the naked and the lazy." Schuyler also used his business and political ties to obtain additional provisions for the army. On 6 October, Montgomery reported that the army was "no longer afraid of starving," and several days later he informed Schuyler to focus on sending soldiers and munitions because he had gathered adequate provisions. Schuyler complied by forwarding reinforcements, heavier weapons, including a 13-inch mortar dubbed the "Old Sow," and different-sized cannonballs to the American forces besieging Saint-Jean, but gunpowder remained in short supply. Equally important, Livingston and approximately 200 Canadians joined Montgomery's command, and they erected a small battery on the east bank of the Richelieu opposite Saint-Jean. This prompted a barrage from the British vessels, but the pro-American Canadians maintained their position.

Several weeks earlier, Montgomery had identified an ideal location to erect a heavy battery and dig approach trenches, a piece of high ground approximately 400 yards west of the northern redoubt. Now that the logistical problems had eased and he had more firepower, the American general intended to press the siege. The proposed battery complemented the one Livingston had built east of Saint-Jean, thus creating a crossfire on the fort. Additionally, British fire would not pose a threat to this location because only one cannon embrasure faced it. Once the battery was operational, the Americans could either batter Saint-Jean into submission or advance close enough to launch an assault once their guns breached the redoubts.

Despite the plan's merits, Montgomery's officers unanimously opposed it at an 11 October council of war. They thought that the ground was too wet to dig trenches and, instead, proposed erecting a battery on the Richelieu's east bank similar to what Livingston had done. Such a battery could not only fire directly into Saint-Jean, but also sink the *Royal Savage*. Montgomery countered that even if the battery destroyed all the fort's buildings, the garrison might not surrender until it faced an assault from the western shore. He also noted that the *Royal Savage* could simply sail away. When his arguments failed to convince the officers, he reluctantly consented to their proposal. Over the next couple of days, 200 soldiers from the 3d New York Regiment built a battery for two 9-pounder cannons on the east side of the Richelieu, about a quarter mile south of Livingston's position. They completed the structure on 13 October.

The new American battery opened fire at 1300 the next day, and their other guns joined the barrage, causing extensive damage to the British works and, more importantly, the *Royal Savage*. One officer recalled, "We shot so many Balls thro her that [the] next morning she lay careen'd so low that the water ran into her port holes." The American barrage continued for the next several days, and the schooner sank on 16 October. Although the garrison showed no signs of surrendering, the *Royal Savage*'s destruction created an opportunity which ultimately proved decisive.

In late September, James Livingston had suggested attacking Fort Chambly—a stone structure 6 miles north of Saint-Jean containing a large quantity of military supplies—but the Americans had not done so. With the *Royal Savage* sunk and the gunpowder shortage becoming more critical, Livingston revived the plan. On 17 October, he and Maj. John Brown surrounded the fort with 350 Continentals and Canadians and opened fire with 2 cannons that Montgomery sent them by way of the Richelieu. The bombardment quickly breached the fort's walls but caused no casualties. Faced with this situation and not knowing that the Americans were nearly out of cannon shot, Maj. Joseph Stopford of the British 7th Regiment of Foot surrendered Chambly the next day, having offered only limited resistance. The presence of a large number of civilians in the fort, many of whom were the families of Saint-Jean's garrison, probably accounted for this. Regardless, the fall of Chambly represented an important turning point in the campaign. In addition to boosting morale, the Americans captured 83 soldiers plus officers, and more importantly 124 barrels of gunpowder, well in excess of 6 tons; 233 muskets; 6,600 cartridges; and a large amount of provisions.

Following a two-day truce to allow for the transportation of the Chambly prisoners and their baggage to Ticonderoga, the Americans resumed their operations against Saint-Jean. Now that he possessed enough ammunition, Montgomery ordered most of his troops west of the Richelieu to begin constructing a battery on a "very advantageous dry piece of ground" north of the fort. From there he could pound Saint-Jean into submission or take it by assault. This was essentially the same plan he had proposed on 11 October, but now his officers proved willing to attempt it. The arrival of badly needed reinforcements aided these efforts. On 24 October, 225 troops from the 4th New York Regiment arrived, followed two days later by the 335 soldiers of the 1st Connecticut Regiment under Wooster, now a brigadier general. This brought the Northern Army's strength to nearly 2,700. Wooster's presence also helped because a New England officer of equal rank to Montgomery now served with the army. Montgomery repeatedly went out of his way to consult with Wooster and even offered to share his quarters with him. The New Englander responded in kind, and the two worked well together, easing intercolonial rivalries.

On the night of 29 October, the Americans began constructing a battery only 250 yards from Saint-Jean, and they completed it the following morning, despite heavy British fire. They then placed four 12-pounder cannons and six mortars in the battery and continued to improve it. A private in Wooster's regiment, 18-year-old Justus Bellamy, recalled carrying six 12-pound cannonballs to the battery in the legs of an old pair of trousers and then picking up a seventh that another soldier dropped. As the Americans made their final preparations, a British deserter from Saint-Jean reported that the garrison was on half rations and desperately short of gunpowder. Even better news came from Longueuil on the St. Lawrence. On 30 October, Col. Seth Warner and 300 Green Mountain Boys and soldiers from the 2d New York Regiment repelled a major British landing to relieve the beleaguered fort. Carleton had gathered 600 militia, 130 regulars, and 80 Native Americans with a large flotilla of bateaux and canoes, but they returned to Montréal after a sharp fight, suffering approximately fifty casualties. Carleton had failed to lift the siege of Saint-Jean.

On the morning of 1 November, the American battery northwest of Saint-Jean opened fire and soon the one east of the Richelieu joined the assault. Over the next 7 hours they fired an estimated 850 solid shots and 120 exploding shells, which caused extensive damage and killed or wounded 8 soldiers. That evening Montgomery sent a message to Preston under a flag of truce carried by a soldier Warner had captured. The American general called upon the garrison to surrender and instructed the prisoner to inform Preston of Carleton's defeat at Longueuil. After brief negotiations, during which the British commander attempted to obtain a four-day delay, Preston agreed to surrender Saint-Jean.

After a 48-day siege, the British soldiers marched out of Saint-Jean and laid down their arms on the morning of 3 November. Justus Bellamy remembered that Preston "cried like a child," saying that he wished that he had not lived to see this day. During the siege, the British had suffered forty killed and wounded, while the Americans had twenty killed, relatively light losses considering the length and intensity of the bombardment.

Saint-Jean was a significant victory. The Americans captured 600 prisoners. These, along with those taken at Chambly, comprised most of the *7th* and *26th Regiments of Foot*, the only regulars in the St. Lawrence Valley. Montgomery's forces also took a large quantity of military and naval supplies and a strategically located fort. The Americans recovered the *Royal Savage* and the row galley, which they named the *Revenge*, and added them to their fleet. Most importantly, they had opened the way to Montréal. One soldier confidently predicted that the victory was "a fatal stab to the hellish machinations of the foes of freedom." Still, Preston and his garrison had bought the British seven weeks with their stubborn defense of the fort, and the weather had turned noticeably colder. With winter fast approaching, the American seizure of the rest of Canada was by no means assured. Although not apparent at the time, Preston had lost the battle but probably won the campaign.

With Saint-Jean now in American hands, Montgomery moved quickly to seize Montréal before Carleton could organize a defense. The heavy wet snow that fell on the night of 3 November demonstrated that time was growing short. Many soldiers believed it was too late in the season to advance deeper into Canada, especially considering their enlistments expired in December. Montgomery defused the situation by promising an early discharge for anyone who wanted to return home after Montréal fell. This convinced most soldiers to continue to serve. The American general then sent Easton and Brown down the Richelieu with a detachment of Massachusetts troops, accompanied by Livingston's Canadians. Montgomery ordered them to disperse Maclean's small British force at the river's mouth, open the Richelieu for American vessels, and cut off any troops retreating from Montréal toward Québec. Maclean retreated toward Québec as Easton approached, so the Americans crossed to the north bank of the St. Lawrence, further isolating Montréal.

Meanwhile, Montgomery and his New Yorkers advanced northwest toward La Prairie on 5 November, followed by Wooster's Connecticut troops. Heavy rains mixed with snow continued to fall, drowning the land and slowing the march. Still, the promise of an early discharge and the prospects of another victory spurred on the soldiers. One wrote, "Under our Feet was Snow and Ice and Water, over our Heads Clouds Snow and rain.... It was remarkable to See the Americans after almost infinite Fatigues and Hardships marching on at this advanced Season, badly clothed, and badly provided for to Montreal."

By 8 November, the Americans had collected thirty bateaux and six cannons at La Prairie, but the poor weather prevented them from crossing to Montréal. Instead, Montgomery sent a letter to its residents urging them to persuade Carleton to surrender, so an American siege would not destroy the city. Montgomery also denied British allegations that his soldiers intended to loot Montréal and cited the army's good behavior up to that time. Three days later, 500 Connecticut and New York soldiers along with Lamb's artillery crossed the St. Lawrence within 3 miles of the city. That same day, Carleton sailed for Québec aboard eleven ships carrying Montréal's small garrison and all the provisions and gunpowder he could collect. The Americans marched to within a mile of the city on 12 November and briefly met with a group of representatives. Montgomery informed them that his army would protect the rights, property, and religion of all Canadians, both French- and English-speaking. With these assurances, the delegates agreed not to resist.

Ten days after taking Saint-Jean, the American Army marched into Montréal. This event held great strategic significance. The largest city in Canada, Montréal was an important trade center and lay astride British supply lines to Fort Niagara, Detroit, and other outposts in the west. The city's capture also enhanced the army's prestige among the Canadians. Increasing numbers enlisted to serve with the Americans, including men from sixteen communities in the Québec district, and Livingston recruited a full regiment for one year. Other inhabitants supplied the Americans with provisions, transportation, and firewood, and a local merchant loaned the army £5,000 in New York currency. Furthermore, Trois-Rivières, the only significant town between Montréal and Québec, sent a delegation to Montgomery acknowledging American control of the region.

Montgomery spent the next fifteen days in Montréal reorganizing his forces and preparing to move against Québec. One of his chief priorities was reenlisting soldiers, especially because their enlistments expired in less than a month. To achieve his goals, he appealed to the soldiers' patriotism. Montgomery thanked them "for their Patience and Perseverance during the Course of a Fatiguing Campaign," but warned that if not enough soldiers reenlisted, all their achievements would be in vain. He also offered material incentives as an additional inducement. Soldiers who reenlisted through 15 April 1776 received a new set of clothing, including a heavy coat, shoes, mittens, and a hat, and a one-dollar cash bounty. Furthermore, Montgomery promised to discharge them earlier if enough reinforcements arrived in Canada. Overall, 800 battle-hardened veterans reenlisted. Although Montgomery had hoped for more, this was enough to garrison Saint-Jean and Montréal and still proceed to Québec.

During this period, Montgomery continued the important diplomatic aspects of the campaign that Schuyler began. On 18–19 September, Montgomery met with seven Kahnawake leaders and obtained their neutrality. Several days later, he presented them with £400 in New York currency, along with gifts for other groups. Additionally, Montgomery repeatedly met with Canadians to gain their support, and he redoubled these efforts after Montréal's fall. The general assured them that the Americans would respect Roman Catholicism and would not negotiate a settlement with Britain unless it also guaranteed Canadian rights. He also tried to organize a convention to select Canadian delegates to the Continental Congress. Montgomery's attempts at persuasion were unsuccessful, partly because Canadians wanted the Americans to take Québec City before they would commit.

Military operations continued while Montgomery prepared for the next phase of the campaign. Easton and Brown erected shore batteries at the mouth of the Richelieu River after dispersing Maclean's troops, and the *Schuyler* and *Hancock* joined them. Carleton's flotilla made several attempts to sail past this position on its way to Québec, but cannon fire drove it back. Meanwhile, Montgomery organized a pursuit from Montréal. Facing capture, Carleton disguised himself as a habitant and escaped to Trois-Rivières in a whaleboat with several others. There, he boarded another ship and arrived at Québec on 20 November. The rest of Carleton's command did not fare as well. Unable to successfully pass the American batteries, on 19 November Brig. Gen. Richard Prescott, who commanded Montréal's garrison, ordered the ships' crews to dump approximately 900 barrels of gunpowder into the river, and he then surrendered. In all, the Americans captured 11 ships along with a large quantity of food, military equipment, and 200 pairs of shoes. They also took nearly 150 prisoners, most of what remained of the *7th* and *26th Regiments of Foot*. This victory marked the peak of American success in Canada, with only Québec City still in British hands.

Arnold's March to Québec

As Schuyler and Montgomery made their first attempts to capture Saint-Jean, Washington organized the expedition against Québec City. He selected Col. Benedict Arnold to lead this mission. Arguably the best American combat officer of the Revolutionary War, Arnold briefly served in the Seven Years' War as a private, and later became a successful Connecticut merchant who developed business ties in both the Caribbean and Canada. Fearless and indefatigable, Arnold always sought action. He seized the gunpowder magazine in New Haven when he heard about Lexington and Concord, and then tried to organize an operation against Fort Ticonderoga before joining Allen's venture. Arnold had lobbied Congress, without success, to command the Montréal expedition before returning to Massachusetts and meeting with Washington. Headstrong and vain, Arnold frequently clashed with other officers, a practice which led to serious problems in the future.

On 5 September, Washington called for volunteers from the Continental Army outside of Boston to participate in a special operation. The following day, he and Arnold picked the soldiers for this mission and organized them into thirteen companies divided into three battalions, approximately 1,100 total. Soldiers from Continental foot regiments made up two of these battalions, and

Arnold's March to Quebec, N. C. Wyeth, 1937 (*Private collection*)

the third consisted of riflemen from Virginia and Pennsylvania. The troops then marched from the Army's camp at Cambridge to Newburyport, where they boarded eleven ships and sailed northeast toward the Kennebec River in Maine on 18 September. After avoiding British warships and battling heavy waves which left many of the soldiers seasick, the fleet arrived at the mouth of the river two days later and proceeded upstream to Gardinerstown. There, they found Reuben Colburn's shipyard and the 200 bateaux that Washington had commissioned. Colburn had rushed to fill the order and therefore used unseasoned or green wood, which later caused major problems as the bateaux leaked excessively. Equally important, the craft were smaller than what Arnold thought was necessary to carry the expedition's 100 tons of equipment and provisions, so he ordered an additional twenty.

Moving upriver to Fort Western—present-day Augusta—Arnold made final preparations. Although Colburn provided him with information about the route, including a map, the colonel also sought his own intelligence by dispatching two advance parties. He ordered the first group of eleven to scout the area, while the second party surveyed the "exact courses and distance to the Dead River" (the western branch of the Kennebec). Additionally, Arnold divided his force into four divisions to depart on successive days. The next day, 25 September, Capt. Daniel Morgan's three companies of riflemen set out with forty-five days' provisions and orders to clear a road for the remaining detachments, which departed as scheduled. Nine St. Francis Indians (a local group of Abenaki who lived near Québec City) handled the canoes with which Arnold traveled from one division to another, and they also served as couriers. In addition, the expedition included at least four wives of enlisted men, two of whom are known by name—Jemima Warner and a Mrs. Grier.

Women regularly accompanied eighteenth-century armies both in camp and in the field. For example, the British Army authorized seven regiments deploying to America in 1775 to take sixty women each. American forces had similar policies both officially and unofficially. Many of these women—usually referred to as camp followers—were married to soldiers, and went with their spouses because of love or because they could not support themselves economically in their husbands' absence. These women were valuable to the armed forces on both sides, most often serving as cooks, laundresses, and nurses. They sometimes received rations for their work. They experienced all the hardships that soldiers did, and in some cases they were killed in combat, but history often does not record their experiences.

Proceeding upstream against the current proved a daunting task, but the expedition gamely persevered. They encountered Ticonic Falls, the first of four on the Kennebec, approximately 20 miles up the river near Fort Halifax (present-day Winslow) and had to portage. Fortunately, Arnold managed to hire local farmers with teams of oxen to help haul the 400-pound bateaux around the half-mile rapid. The boats were too heavy to transport with loads, so the soldiers had to carry all of the provisions and equipment separately, greatly slowing progress. Arnold's soldiers repeated this process many times over the next six weeks, but without the advantage of the oxen once they moved beyond the settled areas. On 7 October, near Norridgewock Falls, 17-year-old Jeremiah Greenman recorded in his journal, "This day [we] left all inhabitants & entered uncultivated country and a barren wilderness."

Eighty-seven miles into the trek on 11 October, the expedition reached the Great Carrying Place, a 12-mile trail that led to the Dead River, so named because of its slow current. Arnold's group spent five days crossing this portage, which included three ponds, a wide swamp, and an ascent of nearly 1,000 feet. By now, so many soldiers had fallen ill that Arnold established a hospital. The soldiers' plight did not improve once they reached the Dead River. Heavy rains and wind, possibly the remains of an Atlantic hurricane, hit on 21–22 October raising the Dead River 8 feet in 8 hours. This flood washed away the camps, destroyed provisions and weapons, and so altered the landscape that it became even more difficult to follow the river's main channel. Six inches of snow fell several days later. Faced with this bleak situation, Arnold held a council of war at which the officers decided to send seventy-five sick soldiers back down the Kennebec. They also sent a party forward to try to reach the French Canadian villages on the Chaudière River to obtain food and transportation. About the same time, Arnold learned that Lt. Col. Roger Enos had—against orders—decided to turn back with the fourth division. This deprived the expedition of most of its remaining provisions and 300 soldiers. Ephraim Stevens, the only African American soldier in Arnold's command, numbered among them.

By this point, Arnold's troops were exhausted. Even though the expedition had a map and an advance party to mark the way, the route remained difficult to follow. The map did not accurately depict all the landmarks and distances through an almost impenetrable maze of streams, forests, and swamps. Pushing and pulling the clumsy, leaky bateaux through icy water, sometimes up to their necks, and then hauling them out of the water and over muddy portages further sapped their strength. Provisions also ran low as rough handling and icy water damaged or destroyed barrels of flour and other food. One veteran remembered, "we suffered greatly before we got through the wilderness; [I] subsisted ten days on a pint of flour." Although Arnold's soldiers obtained fish or game in a few places, most were reduced to eating the dogs who accompanied the expedition, along with squirrel skins, cartridge boxes, bark, candles, and soap.

Arnold's troops struggled on to the headwaters of the Dead River at the Height of Land, crossed this 5-mile highland into Québec, and headed toward Lake Mégantic and the north-flowing Chaudière River, but progress remained slow. Sgt. William McCoy wrote, "This day went astray over mountains and through swamps, which could scarcely be passed by wild beasts. Waded a small river up to our [waists], then marched on. . . . At night we found ourselves within five miles of the place we started from. We marched fifteen miles in vain."

At least two women remained with the expedition. One soldier noted his admiration for the "virtuous and respectable" Mrs. Grier as she waded waist-deep through icy water. Jemima Warner remained behind with her ill husband, and when he died she picked up his rifle and trudged on to catch up with the rest of the expedition.

By early November, Arnold's troops faced starvation, and the weakened soldiers "reeled about like drunken men." Miraculously, on 2 November, the soldiers encountered a group of Canadians driving a small herd of cattle, which they immediately seized and devoured. Arnold, realizing that his expedition was disintegrating, had pressed ahead, braved the wild rapids on the Chaudière, and arrived at the French Canadian settlements at Sartigan on 30 October. He purchased food there and sent it to his emaciated soldiers, along with horses to transport those who could no longer

View of the Falls of the Chaudière, James Peachey, ca. 1784 *(Library and Archives Canada)*

walk. Over the next week, Arnold's ragged command slowly trickled into the settlements, where the habitants welcomed them.

Inaccurate maps and unexpectedly harsh weather and terrain caused Arnold to seriously underestimate the time he needed to complete his epic march, which his contemporaries compared to Hannibal's trek through the Alps. Rather than taking 20 days to cover 180 miles, Arnold's expedition needed 6 weeks to traverse at least 270 miles of wilderness, during which his soldiers made 27 portages on the Kennebec, Dead, and Chaudière Rivers. Of the more than 1,100 who started the expedition, approximately 650 completed it. The rest had deserted, turned back, or died during the ordeal.

Still, Arnold and his intrepid band had arrived in Canada. Over the next ten days he and his troops rested and restored their health, while slowly making their way down the Chaudière. Arnold also planned for the future. He ordered his troops to repair their weapons and build scaling ladders and spears to storm Québec City. He also hired canoes to transport the soldiers to the St. Lawrence and enlisted at least thirty-two Native Americans to join the American cause.

During this period, Arnold heard from Montgomery, who had written him on 29 October from Saint-Jean. Although this letter no longer exists, Montgomery presumably informed Arnold of the situation near Montréal. Over the next few weeks the two officers communicated with each other multiple times by courier—one of whom was a 19-year-old Aaron Burr—and made plans to unite their forces. Arnold's troops very much looked forward to this, because presumably Montgomery could provide them with food, ammunition, and clothing.

On 7 November, Arnold arrived at Pointe-Lévy, near the mouth of the Chaudière River and directly across the St. Lawrence from Québec City, and the rest of his command joined him over the next several days. During this time, he gathered between thirty-five and forty canoes, but heavy winds prevented the Americans from crossing the river. Finally on 13 November, at 2100 approximately 600 of Arnold's troops silently set out, heading for Wolfe's Cove, named for the British general who successfully landed his army there 16 years earlier during the Seven Years' War. Two British warships, HMS *Lizard* and HMS *Hunter*, lay in the middle of the river, but the darkness hid the American craft on their repeated trips. Around 0400, some of Arnold's men exchanged fire with a small boat from the *Lizard*, alerting the ship, but it was too late. The Americans had finished crossing, and they scrambled up the cliffs to the Plains of Abraham west of the city.

With a population of approximately 5,000, Québec City lay where the Saint-Charles River entered the St. Lawrence. The city contained two tiers. The upper town, located atop 300-foot Cape Diamond, held most of the government and religious buildings, and was home primarily to the English-speaking citizens. Thick stone walls, running from the precipice along the St. Lawrence to a bluff skirting the Saint-Charles, encircled it. The walls had four gates, two of which opened on to the Plains of Abraham to the west. A third was located to the north on the Saint-Charles side near the suburb of Saint-Roch, and the last one connected the upper and lower town, which lay at the bottom of Cape Diamond. The lower town, home to most of the original French colonists, contained Québec's docks, warehouses, and many dwellings, but had no walls. Instead, the garrison fortified it with wooden barricades and blockhouses.

On the morning of 14 November, Québec's garrison consisted of more than 1,300 officers and men. This included only 70 regulars from the *7th Regiment of Foot* and *Royal Artillery*, a detachment of 38 marines from the *Lizard*, and 200 *Royal Highland Emigrants* under Maclean, who had arrived at Québec after retreating from the Richelieu River. Two hundred British and 300 Canadian militiamen of questionable loyalty and effectiveness also turned out for service. The sailors from several warships and merchant vessels composed the rest of the garrison, along with eighty "Artificers & Carpenters." Lieutenant Governor Hector T. Cramahé commanded Québec, and he intended to hold the city in Carleton's absence. Although the city's battlements needed repair, they presented a formidable obstacle for the attackers. The fortress also possessed a powerful array of 155 artillery pieces, some of them offloaded from the warships. By the time Arnold crossed the St. Lawrence, Cramahé had mounted at least forty cannons on Québec's walls, including several massive 32-pound guns. Equally important, Québec contained enough provisions to withstand a siege through the spring, when the garrison expected British reinforcements, although it remained short of firewood, hay, and oats.

After arriving on the Plains of Abraham, the Americans occupied several houses and seized some supply carts heading toward the city. Arnold also paraded his troops near Québec and shouted insults at the garrison, hoping to tempt the British out of their fortifications. When this failed, he sent a surrender demand under a flag of truce. The British responded in both cases with several cannon blasts, which scattered the Americans. Although he maintained his position for the next few days, it became increasingly obvious that Arnold lacked the strength to take the city. His soldiers had no cannons, only five musket cartridges each, and little money or adequate clothing. When word arrived that the British intended to launch a surprise attack, Arnold decided to retreat. At 0300 on 19 November, the Americans began a 20-mile march upriver to Pointe-aux-Trembles to await Montgomery. While on the march, they saw

View of Cape Diamond from the River S. Lawrence, George Heriot, ca. 1793 (*Library and Archives Canada*)

a ship on its way to Québec City. Although they did not know it, the vessel carried Carleton, who had just escaped from Montréal.

Meanwhile, Montgomery completed his preparations to advance toward Québec City and join Arnold. The general left Wooster with 500 soldiers to garrison Montréal and the nearby forts, and he sailed on 28 November aboard two of the ships Easton and Brown had captured. Montgomery took 300 soldiers from the 1st, 2d, and 3d New York Regiments and Lamb's artillery company with him, along with 4 cannons, 6 mortars, and new clothing and coats for Arnold's troops. Brown joined Montgomery's force near the mouth of the Richelieu with another 160 soldiers and additional artillery and munitions. Wooster later ordered three additional companies to Québec.

Siege of Québec

On 1 December, Montgomery's ships arrived at Pointe-aux-Trembles, where his and Arnold's commands united (*Map 2*). Montgomery impressed Arnold's troops; one soldier remembered that he delivered a "short, but energetic and elegant speech," thanking them for their service. This welcome breathed "new life . . . into the whole of the corps," and they responded with several "huzzahs." The following day, the general issued new clothing to Arnold's soldiers, including coats taken from British prisoners, and a one-dollar bounty. Montgomery was equally impressed, writing "I find Colonel Arnold's corps an exceedingly fine one, [and] inured to fatigue. . . . There is a style of discipline among them, much superior to what I have been used to see[ing] this campaign." He

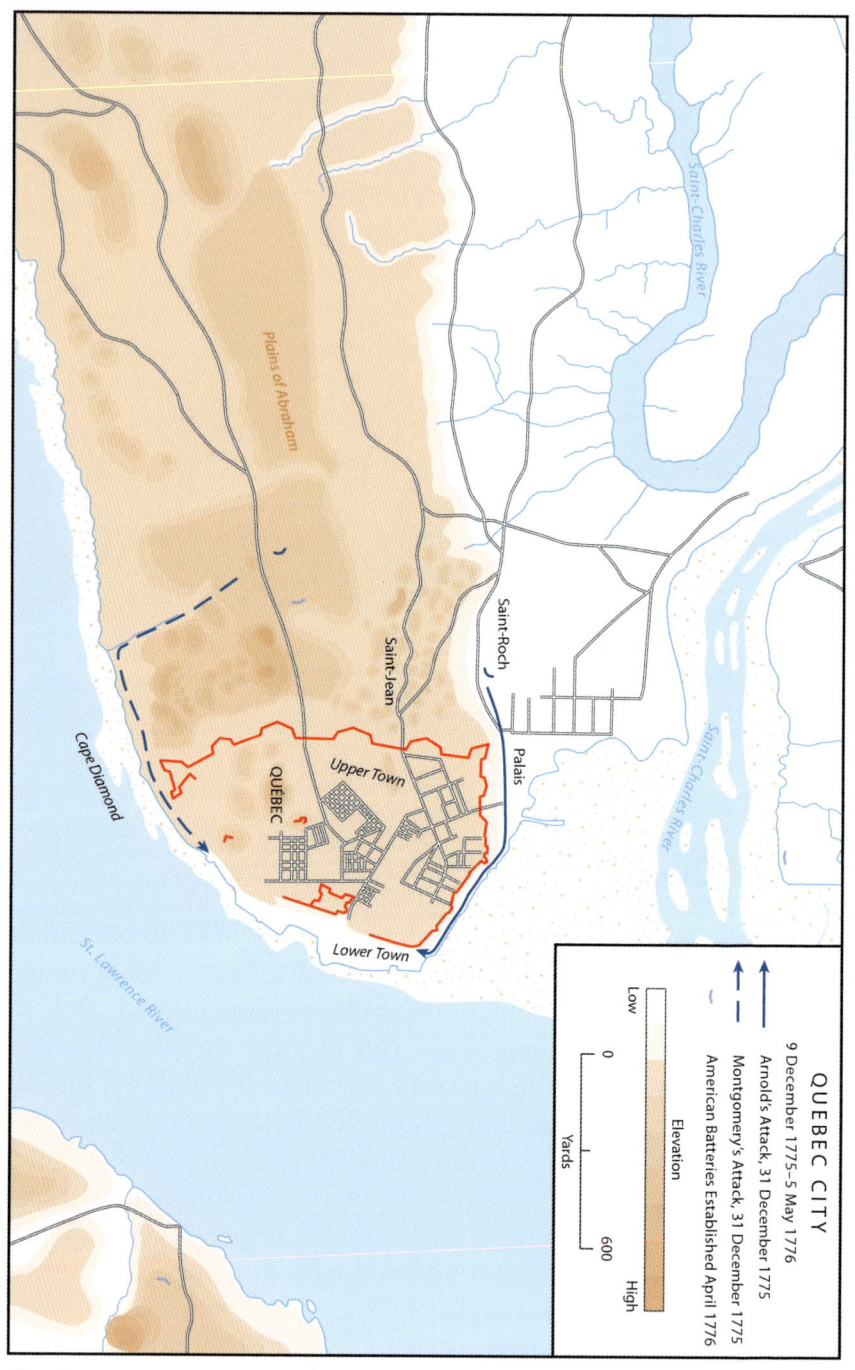

Map 2

also described Arnold as an "active, intelligent, and enterprising" officer, and the two leaders worked well together. Between Montgomery and Arnold, the Americans fielded approximately 1,000 soldiers plus a number of Canadians under Livingston. With their commands united, the Americans returned to Québec, reaching the suburb of Sainte-Foy on 4 December.

Even before arriving at the city, Montgomery had concluded that he probably would have to take Québec by assault. A formal siege was not a viable option because he lacked the firepower to breach the city's wall and the skilled engineers to conduct such an operation. Investment—isolating the city from outside food and fuel—also was not practical because the Americans lacked enough troops to seal off Québec's extensive fortifications effectively. This left assault. In this case, Québec's extensive fortifications would prove detrimental to Carleton because he would have to guard their full expanse all of the time. Montgomery, however, would have the luxury of selecting when and where to attack. Still, Montgomery hesitated to resort to this tactic because of the casualties and destruction that would ensue. Therefore, Montgomery tried other means to take Québec and considered storming the city as a last resort.

Montgomery deployed his soldiers to isolate the city from the surrounding countryside in a vain attempt to starve the garrison. The New Yorkers established themselves near the Plains of Abraham to the west, while Arnold's troops occupied Saint-Roch, near the Saint-Charles River, and erected a battery of six mortars there. The general also sent a detachment to the Île d'Orléans, just down river from Québec, to prevent supplies entering the city from that direction.

The Americans also tried to intimidate Carleton and Québec's residents into surrender. Montgomery sent messages in French and English to Québec's merchants, saying that the Americans came as liberators and not as conquerors who committed atrocities. He urged them to force Carleton to surrender to prevent a destructive siege or assault. He also sent a similar message to Carleton. The governor burned the letter unopened, briefly imprisoned the courier and then released her so she could tell the American general his response. This prompted Montgomery to have the Native Americans with Arnold shoot arrows over the wall with the letter attached.

The Americans also employed more lethal methods to convince Carleton to surrender the city. For several weeks, sharpshooters opened a sporadic yet deadly fire on the battlements, a tactic that outraged the British, who considered it cowardly and deceitful. One militia officer wrote, "They are worse than Savages, [and] they will ever be held in contempt with men of courage. Lie in wait to shoot a sentry! a deed worthy of Yanky men of war." Additionally, the Saint-Roch mortar battery opened fire on 10 December and continued to lob shells into the upper town through the end of the month. Montgomery similarly ordered his troops to construct a siege battery 700 yards from Québec on the Plains of Abraham, but frigid weather and heavy snow prevented them from digging entrenchments. The Americans improvised by throwing water on snow-filled fascines and *gabions*—wooden baskets filled with dirt used for earthworks or to protect troops while entrenching—so that they would freeze solid. By 15 December, Montgomery's soldiers, under Lamb's direction, had completed the ice battery, which held five 12-pounder cannons and a howitzer.

The battery opened fire for an hour that morning, after which Montgomery sent Carleton a final message under a flag of truce. The American general offered the governor safe passage to England if he would surrender, but Carleton again refused to acknowledge the letter. The battery then resumed fire, but the distance was too great, and Montgomery's guns lacked the weight to destroy Québec's fortifications. The mortar battery in Saint-Roch produced similar results, and these events actually improved British morale by reassuring Québec's residents of the ineffectiveness of the Americans' bombardment.

Furthermore, the British counterbattery fire proved brutally effective. Earlier in the month, British cannons had inflicted a number of American casualties, including killing the intrepid Jemima Warner, who had trekked through the wilderness with Arnold's command and remained with it following her husband's death. British gunners now concentrated their fire on the

American ice battery. Over the next two days, 32-pound solid shots demolished the structure, dismounted its cannons, and killed their crews, causing the Americans to abandon the shattered works. Montgomery actually saw some benefits arising from the ice battery's quick destruction. He had built it mainly to hide his true plans from Carleton. As Montgomery informed his father-in-law, "It may indeed be of service by giving the Enemy security—and Security dwells next door to destruction."

Having failed to induce Québec to surrender, Montgomery made plans to assault the city. Time was an issue because the enlistments of many in Arnold's forces expired on 1 January 1776, and the American general doubted that most would stay beyond that date. When he first had arrived, Montgomery tentatively had decided to storm the less-fortified lower town. He then received intelligence from disaffected outcasts whom Carleton had expelled from Québec City for not serving with the British. These individuals informed Montgomery that the lower town's vulnerability especially concerned the British, and they had strengthened its defenses. This prompted the American general to switch his attention to the upper town, and by mid-December he had decided to launch a night assault during a heavy snowstorm to cover his soldiers' approach. One-third of the assault force would attack the lower town after setting fire to some houses near Saint-Roch to create a diversion and disrupt the British defenses. The rest would storm the Cape Diamond bastion in the upper town by escalade—with ladders to mount the walls—forcing Carleton to defend both parts of Québec simultaneously. Montgomery planned this attack for Christmas Eve, but canceled it after a British prisoner escaped into Québec and delivered this news to the garrison.

Dissension in Arnold's command further complicated the planned assault. During this period, Montgomery learned that three of Arnold's captains had clashed repeatedly with their commander over a variety of issues and now wanted to detach as a separate command. They also seemed unwilling to participate in an attack. Montgomery listened to their complaints but did not detach them from Arnold's command. Still, his consideration somewhat mollified the three captains. Montgomery took an even more important step by also meeting with Arnold's troops to quell any dissent and gain their support. On 25 December, he delivered a short but powerful appeal in which he invoked the valor that they had displayed on their rugged march to Québec. Montgomery assured them that the attack would succeed if they exhibited this spirit again. He finished by promising that victory would secure Canada for the American cause, bring liberty to its residents, and ensure the soldiers' "immortal honor." One recalled that they answered Montgomery "with a cheer," and another wrote that "the fire of patriotism kindled in our breasts, and we resolved to follow wherever he should lead."

With this situation now resolved, Montgomery again planned an attack for the night of 27 December. A storm began to develop that afternoon, but never materialized, causing the general to cancel the assault again. The delay had far-reaching consequences. That night, two soldiers deserted into Québec, and they gave Montgomery's assault plan to Carleton. The next day, the American general learned from spies that the British had redeployed their forces to repel an attack against the Cape Diamond bastion.

Montgomery had no choice but to change his plans and again direct his efforts toward the lower town instead of the upper one. Arnold would still attack from Saint-Roch, in line with Montgomery's original plan, but would now have his entire command and Lamb's artillery rather than just one third of the Northern Army. Meanwhile, Montgomery would attack the lower town from the opposite side with his New Yorkers, using a path that ran along the St. Lawrence at the foot of Cape Diamond. The two columns would then meet. Having secured Québec's commercial district, they could then either fight their way into the upper town, or perhaps convince Carleton to surrender, if the city's merchants did not do so first. The new plan also provided for two feints against the upper town to confuse the garrison. Livingston's Canadians would set fire to Saint John's Gate, which opened to the Plains of Abraham, and demonstrate there, while a small force led by Capt. Jacob Brown launched a diversionary attack at the Cape Diamond bastion. Brown also had orders to fire signal rockets to create more confusion and alert the other columns that the attack had commenced. Brown's and Livingston's commands then would assist the main columns as much as possible, depending on how the garrison reacted.

The opportunity to implement the new plan came on the night of 30–31 December when a howling blizzard descended on Québec. The storm created the ideal conditions for the assault and proved timely, considering that Arnold's enlistments expired the next day. Montgomery ordered the army to assemble by 0200 and attack at 0500. Although some confusion ensued, the soldiers appeared enthusiastic as they prepared for combat and marched to their rendezvous sites. They wore hemlock sprigs in their hats to identify themselves, and many also attached pieces of paper bearing the words "Liberty or Death."

The four American columns set out early in the morning of 31 December. Montgomery led between 250 and 300 New Yorkers, whereas Arnold had 600 soldiers and a 6-pounder cannon. Brown led another 100 soldiers, and Livingston's Canadians were about twice that number.

The diversion on the upper town began between 0400 and 0500 when Brown fired two signal rockets and opened heavy musket fire on the Cape Diamond bastion. This prompted the British sentries to sound the alarm and return fire. Livingston's troops soon appeared near Saint John's Gate and tried to burn it, while the mortar battery in Saint-Roch opened fire.

Montgomery's troops faced the longest and most difficult approach that morning. They marched southwest for 1 mile, descended the heights to Wolfe's Cove, and then turned east for 2 miles along a narrow, icy path covered with several feet of snow at the base of the cliff. Heavy snow, propelled by gale-force winds, further hindered their approach, as did the darkness and bitter cold. The column was soon badly extended and was not in position to attack when Brown began his diversion against the upper town. They pushed on, however, and about half an hour before dawn they reached the lower town's outer works, two 15- to 20-foot-high palisades near the point of Cape Diamond.

Montgomery personally led the column as his forces cut their way through both palisades. Thus far, the garrison seemed unaware of their presence on the outskirts of the lower town. As they emerged from the second barricade, the soldiers discovered one last obstacle—a two-story blockhouse that appeared empty. Montgomery ordered his troops forward, only to be met by a withering barrage of grapeshot from the soldiers and artillery hidden in the building. The blast killed the general and most of the soldiers around him, disheartening his command. Col. Donald Campbell briefly attempted to rally the soldiers, but it was no use. With the element of surprise long gone, Montgomery dead, and many weapons inoperable because of the wet snow, Campbell ordered a retreat. This eliminated one of the two main assault forces and allowed the British to turn their efforts toward the other side of the lower town.

At approximately the same time, Arnold's troops, some carrying scaling ladders, marched toward the lower town from Saint-Roch. Arnold led the way, but the path was so narrow that they had to march in single file. His advance guard of twenty-five soldiers preceded Lamb's artillery company, which dragged their cannon with them on a sled. The rest of his troops followed behind the artillerymen. The heavy, blowing snow quickly covered their footprints, making it difficult for others to follow them. One soldier recalled, "The storm was outrageous, and the cold wind extremely biting. In this northern country the snow is blown horizontally into the faces of travellers on most occasions—this was our case." The snow became so deep that Lamb finally had to abandon the gun. The British then discovered the column as it passed one of the city's gates, and they opened a heavy fire from above, killing and wounding several Americans. At this point, church bells began to toll in Québec, sounding a general alarm.

Arnold's advance guard then encountered a 10-foot-high wooden barricade mounted with two cannons that blocked their passage into the lower town. Early in the ensuing short, sharp fight, a musket ball hit Arnold in the left leg, and he left the field, bleeding heavily. Capt. Daniel Morgan assumed command, as some soldiers fired through the gunports at the British troops beyond, and others mounted the

Arnold's Column Is Shattered in Fierce Street Fighting During the Battle of Quebec, Charles Williams Jeffreys, 1916 (Wikimedia Commons)

barricade with scaling ladders. The Americans quickly overran the position, rounding up approximately thirty prisoners.

Arnold's troops were now in the Sault-au-Matelot, a narrow street with Cape Diamond on one side and the frozen St. Lawrence on the other. Morgan rushed ahead to a second barricade and found it undefended, but the American attack unraveled. The prisoners they had taken slowed them down and many of the soldiers' weapons would no longer fire because of the wet snow. Even worse, the combination of the snow and the British fire coming from above slowed the movement of the rear of the column. Instead of pushing forward, Morgan waited for his missing support to arrive.

For the next several hours, the Americans occupied some buildings in the lower town, dried and reloaded their firearms, and exchanged gunfire with the rapidly growing number of British soldiers on the far side of the second barricade. Some of Arnold's soldiers also ventured out onto the St. Lawrence's ice trying to outflank the British position but to no avail. Initially, the Americans believed that they were winning, as they heard musket and cannon fire coming from other parts of the town, and some shouted "Québec is ours." This was not the case. Québec's garrison had repelled Livingston quickly at Saint John's Gate and realized that Brown's diversion posed no real danger. With Montgomery's repulse, Carleton sent reinforcements to the lower town, and the British encircled Morgan's troops. Two sixty-man detachments attacked the rear of Morgan's position and cut off his retreat. By midmorning, Morgan realized that Montgomery's command was not coming, and that the British had surrounded him. Faced with this situation, he and most of his command reluctantly surrendered.

The 31 December assault on Québec was an unmitigated disaster for the American Army in Canada. It lost 48 killed—including Montgomery and 5 other officers—34 wounded, and 372 captured, including much of Arnold's command, which largely surrendered en masse. Carleton added to the victory by overrunning the American battery in Saint-Roch and seizing six cannons and mortars, along with some ammunition. British casualties included five dead and fourteen wounded, only one of which proved serious. Montgomery's death deprived the Americans of strong, steady leadership for the remainder of their efforts in Canada, but it made him one of the war's first martyrs.

In the days immediately following the failed assault, both Arnold and Campbell sent letters to Wooster about the disaster and requested immediate reinforcements. On 14 January, Wooster sent 120 New York soldiers to Québec from Montréal, and he dispatched 70 more the following week. Wooster, however, did not personally travel to Québec until late March because of his age and other responsibilities. He asked Seth Warner, who had returned home with his Green Mountain Boys after Montréal's fall, to send a further contingent of 500 as soon as possible, even if they arrived in small detachments.

Wooster forwarded the news of the defeat and Montgomery's death to Schuyler, Washington, and Congress, and requested reinforcement. Congress ordered Washington to send a battalion to Canada without delay, and it instructed two New Jersey and

Pennsylvania regiments, which it had assigned previously to march north, to deploy whatever troops were ready. Both Congress and Washington later expanded on these efforts, but it took time for substantial numbers of fresh troops to arrive in Canada. The first new Continental soldiers—several Pennsylvania companies—did not reach Montréal until 18 February, and they were not fully equipped. By mid-March, fewer than 1,500 new soldiers had reached Canada, and Lake Champlain had begun to thaw, temporarily stopping further reinforcements until the rotten ice cleared.

Meanwhile, Arnold nursed his wounded leg and gamely maintained the blockade of Québec as best he could. Following the assault, he had fewer than 800 troops, about half of whom were Canadians. Still, his soldiers managed to prevent most supplies from getting into the city, and 6-foot snow drifts aided his efforts by making the road impassable. Arnold attempted to increase his numbers by recruiting more Canadians, and he authorized Jeremiah Duggan, who had assisted James Livingston, to raise a regiment. He requested additional muskets from Montréal to arm them, and eventually requisitioned them from local citizens. These efforts enjoyed some success, and other Canadians aided the Americans in a variety of ways. Some sold them provisions while others stood guard and provided them with intelligence. In several cases, women—sometimes dubbed "Queens of Hungary" (a reference to Maria-Theresa of Austria)—proved to be staunch supporters of the American cause. In Saint-Vallier, east of Québec on the south shore, a widow named Gabourie "caused more harm in this parish than anyone" when she held frequent meetings where she "raised the people's spirits against the government and urged them to side with the rebels." The wife of a man named Augustin Chabot similarly "perverted almost all the people by spreading her seditious remarks as she went door to door" on Île d'Orléans.

Still, the American position in Canada eroded because of several persistent problems. Throughout the revolution, the Americans used a confusing variety of currencies—both paper and coins (referred to then as specie)—issued by individual colonies and Congress. Whether denominated in pounds or dollars, money remained in short supply throughout the campaign. Montgomery's army had only limited cash when it arrived in Canada, and Arnold's troops lost their barrel of specie on the march through the wilderness. Montgomery later borrowed additional money from a Montréal merchant, but by winter and spring 1776, this amount was largely exhausted. Without funds, it was difficult to pay soldiers and buy provisions for maintaining the army. Initially, the Americans used paper money and issued receipts which Arnold promised to redeem for specie in four months. The Canadians were skeptical of these paper promises, remembering similar experiences with French troops in the Seven Years' War, and they were reluctant to accept receipts from the American soldiers. This undercut their support of the army. By the spring of 1776, the Americans had accumulated debts of $14,000 with no way of paying them back, and this shortfall became worse as reinforcements arrived in Canada. Lacking provisions, soldiers often confiscated what they needed, further alienating civilians and hurting army discipline. These shortages, which included reductions in diet, also made the soldiers more susceptible to disease.

Schuyler tried to address this lack of money and provisions as best he could, at times drawing upon his personal resources. He used his own credit so Wooster could purchase blankets and other goods in March, and "collected on my notes, payable in like money," almost £2,140 in hard currency. Schuyler also sent 400 barrels of pork by sled to the Northern Army in Canada, at considerable expense, and looked into the cost-effectiveness of driving livestock there. He continued these efforts throughout the spring, requesting artillery stores, clothing, and gunpowder from Continental warehouses in New York City. In the first week of June, Schuyler sent 450 barrels of pork, 187 of flour, and 40 of corn northward, but this proved insufficient in the end. Some provisions spoiled, soldiers and bateaux crews mishandled or lost others, and the army had a great need for supplies and equipment.

Longstanding civilian-military issues further added to the Northern Army's woes. Throughout the fall, Montgomery had requested that Congress send a delegation to establish formal ties with Canada and oversee various administrative activities. Congress attempted this in November 1775, but the delegation traveled no farther than Fort Ticonderoga before returning to Philadelphia. Therefore, Montgomery and later Wooster, had to contend with such issues as negotiating with local tribes, handling security questions concerning loyalists, and dealing with a host of other civil governance issues, in addition to conducting military operations. Montgomery had managed to handle these challenges for the short term when the Americans enjoyed military success, but they became more pressing the longer the army remained in Canada.

Through early 1776, Wooster struggled to resolve the issues but angered many Canadians in the process, both those who supported and opposed the Americans. He ordered the arrest and removal to the colonies of some Montréal residents who maintained ties to the British government and now posed potential security threats. Although pro-American Canadians welcomed this move, and had even encouraged it, others viewed the arrests as arbitrary and contrary to the army's claims of coming as liberators. Similarly, that spring Montréal fur traders requested that the general issue licenses so they could send trade items to the Great Lakes. Wooster refused, fearing that these goods might end up at British military posts. He claimed that he needed congressional approval to issue the licenses, but Congress was in far-away Philadelphia.

In mid-February, Congress finally authorized a new delegation composed of Benjamin Franklin, Samuel Chase, and Charles Carroll, the last accompanied by his cousin John Carroll, a Catholic priest. Congress charged the committee with settling issues related to the American occupation of Canada, but it did not arrive in Montréal until 29 April. The committee also brought $20,000 in paper Continental currency, not specie, which did little to reassure the Canadians or satisfy the Northern Army's creditors. In June, Congress authorized sending $22,000 in silver to the army, but by that time it was far too late.

Smallpox presented the biggest and deadliest threat to the American Army in Canada. Endemic to the St. Lawrence Valley, the first cases of this disease appeared in the army besieging Québec in December. By 12 February, Arnold reported that 250 of his 800 soldiers were sick, including 50 with smallpox. The outbreak grew to epidemic proportions, especially as additional reinforcements arrived in Canada. Part of the problem was that many soldiers self-inoculated with the virus, hoping to contract a milder version of the dreaded disease, but these preventative efforts left even more soldiers ill. Officers tried to isolate those infected, but this often proved impossible, ineffective, or they discovered the infected too late. By the end of February, the Americans had quarantined 100 soldiers with the disease at Québec, and hundreds more joined them over the coming weeks. One of Warner's soldiers wrote, "many died of the small pox, severe cold, hardships, and privation during the winter." Another, John Train, recalled that between March and May, his captain and lieutenant died of the "spotted fever" (typhus) and two sergeants and six privates died from smallpox. In May, an American officer reported that of the 2,000 soldiers at Québec, 1,200 were unfit for duty, mainly because of smallpox.

Over the course of the winter, Carleton had done little, aside from remaining alert in Québec and waiting for reinforcements, as the American situation in Canada deteriorated. In March, he began to encourage pro-British Canadians to resist. The British governor sent a secret message to a seigneur, Louis-Liénard de Beaujeu de Villemomble, to gather loyalist residents on the south shore of the St. Lawrence and attack the American position at Pointe-Lévy. By 24 March, Beaujeu had raised approximately 150 recruits and sent an advance guard of approximately 40 to the village of Saint-Pierre-du-Sud, where they raised the British flag. Pro-American Canadians discovered this threat, however, and informed Arnold, who sent eighty Continentals to Pointe-Lévy. The Americans met approximately fifty friendly Canadians, and they marched toward Saint-Pierre, gathering additional support as they went. On 25 March, the Americans and their allies surrounded the loyalists' position undetected and routed them in a short skirmish. The Americans killed three loyalists, wounded ten, and captured the rest, at the cost of only one wounded. When Beaujeu learned of this defeat, he quickly retreated and his force disbanded, ending the threat of a loyalist uprising on the south bank. Although the skirmish at Saint-

Pierre resulted in an American success, it showed some Canadians' increased willingness to support the British openly.

As American troop strength at Québec slowly grew, Arnold renewed his efforts to take the city. He ordered his soldiers to erect batteries at Pointe-Lévy and on the Plains of Abraham where the ice battery had stood, and both became operational by the first week of April. Arnold later began to construct an additional battery on the far side of the Saint-Charles River, and an increasing number of small skirmishes occurred between American pickets and British foraging parties searching for firewood.

Arriving at the city on 1 April, Wooster assumed responsibilities for the siege as the ranking officer. He sought little advice or input from Arnold and subsequently granted him permission to go to Montréal, where he could contribute to the American effort. One of Wooster's first actions was to authorize the preparation of a fireship to destroy the British naval vessels near Québec. He also had to deal with expiring enlistments, as the soldiers that Montgomery had recruited in Montréal the previous fall completed their term of service on 15 April. These troops represented 60 percent of the soldiers at Québec. Wooster proved unable to entice most of them to reenlist but, through a series of orders and administrative delays, managed to keep most of them at Québec for an additional two weeks. This tactic allowed time for additional reinforcements to arrive.

Maj. Gen. John Thomas, whom Congress appointed to command in Canada following Montgomery's death, also arrived at Québec during this time. A surgeon by training, Thomas had participated in the recently concluded siege of Boston, which resulted in the British evacuating that city on 17 March. He then set out for Canada, passing through Montréal on 26 April and pushing on to Québec, where he arrived six days later. Now that the ice had cleared from Lake Champlain, soldiers poured into Canada. Thomas headed approximately 6,000 troops. From the Hudson River to the Richelieu and Québec, regiments from New Hampshire, Massachusetts, Pennsylvania, and New Jersey marched north. Although the Northern Army welcomed these fresh soldiers, they frequently lacked adequate arms, munitions, and even medicine. They also requisitioned provisions from civilians on their way to Québec, which did nothing to help the American cause. Furthermore, these troops became entangled with those returning to the colonies as their enlistments expired. Even worse, many of the arriving soldiers quickly contracted smallpox, both through natural means and inoculations. Arnold had allowed the latter practice, but Thomas halted it, although he lacked immunity, having never had the disease himself. Soon after Thomas's arrival, the Americans launched their fireship, but alert British sailors spotted the vessel and diverted it from their anchorage before it caused any damage.

Thomas also evaluated the army before Québec and consulted with his officers. Short on provisions and with more than half of his soldiers ill, Thomas decided to lift the blockade and retreat upriver about 40 miles to Deschambault, where he hoped to obstruct any British advance. Just as the Americans began to prepare for this move, the situation changed dramatically.

Retreat From Canada

On the evening of 5 May, signal fires from the south shore of the St. Lawrence indicated the arrival of British warships. At 0500, three vessels—the vanguard of a much larger relief force totaling approximately 12,000 British and German soldiers and sailors commanded by Maj. Gen. John Burgoyne—arrived at Québec City. The warships unloaded troops from the *29th Regiment of Foot* and a detachment of marines. Several hours later, Carleton and 800 soldiers—many newly arrived—sortied from the city. The American Army, already beginning to withdraw, offered little resistance, and then precipitously fled. It abandoned many weapons (including cannons captured the previous November at Saint-Jean), equipment, and clothing. It also left behind many of the sick and wounded, while the troops at Pointe-Lévy and Île d'Orléans did not receive orders to retreat. They had to make their way to the main Northern Army on their own. The next morning, 7 May, British warships attacked American vessels in the St. Lawrence, capturing many bateaux, including one containing tons of gunpowder and muskets, and sinking the *Schuyler* and *Hancock*. They also fired grapeshot at retreating American soldiers.

The army briefly reformed at Deschambault, but Thomas doubted that it could withstand a British attack. He ordered the retreat to continue 85 miles to the mouth of the Richelieu River, where the Americans evacuated the north side of the St. Lawrence. Thomas proposed to make a stand at Sorel where he could cooperate with Arnold's forces in Montréal and newly arriving troops. These included Brig. Gen. William Thompson's brigade—Cols. Enoch Poor's 8th, John Paterson's 15th, John Greaton's 24th, and William Bond's 25th Continental Regiments—which had arrived in Canada on 13 May. Fortunately, Carleton did not pursue the Americans aggressively, partly because of logistical problems. One of the four supply ships of the relief fleet burned before it sailed, depriving the vanguard of much of its provisions. The Americans had also stripped the area of most foodstuffs during the siege. Therefore, Carleton issued a proclamation encouraging Canadians to deliver any sick or wounded Americans to him. Once these "deluded subjects" had regained their health, Carleton promised to send them home, thereby portraying Britain as a benevolent ruler and undercutting American resolve.

Although Carleton did not pose an immediate threat, one had developed west of Montréal. On 12 May, Capt. George Forster, commander of the British outpost at present-day Ogdensburg, New York, began a 120-mile advance toward Montréal with 40 regulars from the *8th Regiment of Foot*, 11 Canadians, and 160 Mississauga and Iroquois. Additional Native Americans and Canadians later joined Forster, and on 18 May, he approached the Cedars, also known as Fort Cedars, an American outpost, approximately 25 miles west of Montréal, garrisoned by 350 New Hampshire soldiers and supported by 2 cannons. On 19 May, Forster encircled the position, and intimidated its commander, Maj. Isaac Butterfield, into surrender by threatening an Indian massacre. The next day, some of Forster's troops ambushed a relief force of 100 soldiers led by Maj. Henry Sherburne and forced it to surrender after a short battle. In these two actions, Forster killed or captured approximately 450 soldiers, including several African Americans, one of whom, Primus Chandler, was never seen again. Forster now posed a direct threat to Montréal. As he advanced toward Lachine, about 8 miles west of the city, however, some of his Native Americans and Canadians returned home with their plunder, diminishing his numbers.

When Arnold learned of the two defeats, he gathered 350 Continentals and marched to Lachine, hoping to defeat Forster and liberate the prisoners. Upon learning of the large force opposing him, Forster began to retreat with his numerous captives. With the addition of reinforcements that increased his strength to nearly 500, Arnold rapidly pursued them. At this point, Forster quickly negotiated a prisoner exchange with Butterfield and Sherburne, whereby he would release the Americans in exchange for future British prisoners. On 26 May, Sherburne sent a flag of truce to Arnold explaining the agreement, which the latter initially refused to accept. After some negotiations, which included a four-day truce, Arnold acquiesced. Forster used the cease-fire to escape with his force. Overall, the fighting at the Cedars represented another embarrassment for the Continental Army and illustrated its collapse in Canada in May 1776.

Further evidence of this breakdown soon followed. On 21 May, General Thomas contracted smallpox, and he died on 2 June. Wooster was now the ranking American officer in Canada, but the congressional committee found great fault with his abilities and recommended his recall. Wooster convened a council of war on 30 May at Chambly, where the gathered officers decided to continue to hold their position but make plans to evacuate Canada. Exhausted by his service and stung by the criticism, Wooster then returned to the colonies, as did the committee, leaving Thompson in command.

Around this time, Thompson received intelligence that Carleton's advance guard of approximately 300 had arrived at Trois-Rivières. With numerous fresh troops available, including his own, he decided to counterattack with 600 Pennsylvanians. Before this could occur, however, Brig. Gen. John Sullivan arrived in Canada with his brigade. Large numbers of Canadians greeted them, showing that the Americans still enjoyed some support. Sullivan learned of Thomas's death and, as the highest-ranking general in Canada, found himself in command. After a quick evaluation of additional intelligence, he expanded upon Thompson's initial plan and ordered him to attack Trois-Rivières with nearly 1,800 New Jersey and Pennsylvania troops.

Divided into five separate detachments, Thompson's soldiers loaded into bateaux and landed 7 miles above Trois-Rivières on 7 June, planning to surprise the British with a swift attack. The American force set out with a guide, but quickly became lost in a dense swamp. When the muddy, exhausted troops finally arrived at Trois-Rivières hours later, they immediately came under fire from British warships. Furthermore, Thompson's troops found nearly 2,000 entrenched soldiers supported by artillery waiting for them, instead of a small advance guard. The British easily repelled the disjointed assaults and then counterattacked, driving the Americans back to their landing site and ultimately to Sorel. The Battle of Trois-Rivières cost the Northern Army approximately 400 soldiers, including Thompson and 236 other prisoners. British combined losses totaled about a dozen.

Sullivan faced a grim prospect as the survivors of the Trois-Rivières debacle arrived at Sorel. With the army ravaged by smallpox, a lack of provisions, and collapsing morale, the Americans would have to evacuate Canada. Arnold, in Montréal, had recently come to the same conclusion. "I am heartily chagrined to think we have lost in one month all the immortal Montgomery was a whole campaign in gaining, together with our credit, and many men, and an amazing sum of money." On 14 June, Sullivan ordered his soldiers to retreat from Sorel to Chambly and then to Saint-Jean. The Americans abandoned twenty cannons and burned three small warships at Chambly, before struggling to haul bateaux filled with equipment, provisions, and sick soldiers over the rapids on the Richelieu. They then continued their retreat.

Carleton's actions added to the urgency. On 14 June, thirty-six British vessels arrived at Sorel. The following morning, Burgoyne, Carleton's second-in-command, landed with 4,000 soldiers and began marching south, but they could not overtake Sullivan's column. Meanwhile, Carleton headed for Montréal with the fleet. He planned to retake the city, cross the St. Lawrence at Longueuil and La Prairie, and then march rapidly overland to Saint-Jean, using the same route Montgomery had taken the previous November. This would put Carleton behind Sullivan, trapping the American Army in Canada. On 15 June, Arnold learned that Sullivan had retreated from Sorel and that British ships were approaching Montréal, but fortunately contrary winds delayed them. By the next day, Arnold had evacuated the 300 soldiers in the city's garrison, taking all the provisions and equipment he could and destroying the rest. He then crossed to the south shore of the St. Lawrence, burned his bateaux, and set out for Saint-Jean, destroying bridges behind him in an attempt to slow Carleton. On 17 June, Arnold's and Sullivan's commands reunited at Saint-Jean, where the officers decided to retreat to Île-aux-Noix. Several hundred Canadians—both Old and New Subjects—accompanied the Americans on their retreat. Many of them, including Edward Chinn and his "slave for life" John Saratoga, served with the 2d Canadian Regiment later in the war. The American soldiers burned Saint-Jean's shipyard, pried two tons of lead from a roof to make musket balls, and sailed away the next evening, taking four warships with them. The fiery Arnold was the last of the Americans to leave. Burgoyne's troops arrived soon after, as did Carleton's the next morning.

The 5,000 American and Canadian soldiers who made it to the 210-acre Île-aux-Noix on 18–19 June came from at least sixteen different regiments, but unit integrity had broken down. Smallpox and other maladies had stricken thousands of officers and enlisted men, and the army lacked enough doctors and medicine to treat them. Some soldiers were fortunate to have tents but many lay in the open, and the island's few trees provided little shade. Provisions remained in short supply as did potable water, and over the next twelve days hundreds of soldiers died. One physician wrote, "No mortal will ever believe what these [soldiers] suffered unless they were eye witnesses." Sullivan knew the army's position was untenable and started to evacuate the sick to Crown

Point 90 miles farther south, with the first leaving on 20 June. He lacked enough bateaux to transport them all at once, forcing the exhausted boat crews to make multiple round trips in the hot summer sun. The rest of the army then followed. The last battered, disease-wracked remnants of the Northern Army finally arrived at Crown Point on 2 July, at least salvaging some of the force from the disastrous campaign.

Rebuilding the Northern Army

Maj. Gen. Horatio L. Gates, whom Congress appointed to command the Northern Army after Thomas's death, was also at Crown Point that day. Over the next four months, Gates, with strong assistance from Schuyler, Arnold, and many others, successfully rebuilt the Northern Army. Schuyler and Gates's relationship proved a critical factor that allowed this to occur. Congress had appointed Gates to command in Canada, but by the time he joined the army, it was in New York. This situation raised the question of who was to command the soldiers, Gates or Schuyler. The two quickly agreed that Schuyler would remain in overall command of the Northern Department, while Gates assumed tactical command of the Northern Army at Ticonderoga, a decision that Congress reaffirmed. This decision allowed Gates to concentrate on the immediate task of restoring the army, while Schuyler used his logistical skills to supply him with fresh troops, equipment, medicine, provisions, and other supplies.

One of Gates and Schuyler's first and most important decisions involved selecting a location at which to make a stand on Lake Champlain. They ultimately chose Ticonderoga, not only because of its defensive potential, but also because, unlike Crown Point, smallpox had not yet appeared there. Over the next several weeks, healthy soldiers marched south to Ticonderoga, while bateaux transported those infected with smallpox to Fort George on Lake George. There, 29-year old Dr. Jonathan Potts oversaw what became the largest hospital in North America, a facility which at times held nearly 3,000 patients. A number of women from Pennsylvania regiments at Ticonderoga served as nurses at this hospital. By late summer, Potts and his overworked staff managed to contain the smallpox epidemic and actually return soldiers to the army.

Meanwhile, Gates implemented a whole series of initiatives to rebuild the Northern Army and its morale. He began by restoring discipline. He reestablished the chain of command, had regiments again keep orderly books listing each day's standing orders, and implemented floggings for serious offenses. He assigned the New England, Pennsylvania, and New Jersey soldiers to separate areas around Ticonderoga to reduce intercolonial friction. With Schuyler's assistance, he also provided the soldiers with new uniforms, shoes, blankets, and other articles of clothing. On 30 July, the army received 1,108 shirts and 631 pairs of shoes and moccasins, and similar shipments continued. The Commissary Department, ably led by Joseph Trumbull, purchased and delivered large amounts of beef, flour, and other foodstuffs, while local farmers established markets at which the troops could buy fresh fruits and vegetables.

In addition to providing for the soldiers' material well-being, Gates kept them busy with drills and defense improvements around Ticonderoga. The Northern Army's chief engineer, Col. Jeduthan Baldwin, designed a complex series of inner and outer fortifications that the troops spent the summer building. The most notable of these was the construction of Mount Independence, a powerful bastion directly opposite Ticonderoga on the east shore of Lake Champlain. Between Ticonderoga and Mount Independence, the Americans blocked the passage to the upper end of the lake at Skenesborough. Gates assisted the soldiers by obtaining skilled carpenters, blacksmiths, and other artisans who helped improve Ticonderoga's defenses.

Overall, the reforms that Gates and the others instituted revitalized the Northern Army. So did the arrival of additional Continental and militia regiments, many of which included African American soldiers, such as Lemuel Haynes, a veteran of the siege of Boston, who later became a Congregationalist minister in New York and Vermont. By 24 August, Gates reported that he had nearly 8,000 present for duty at Ticonderoga, Crown Point, and Skenesborough, including a company of Stockbridge Mohican scouts. This represented a dramatic improvement from the 2,400 available in early July. At the core of the army were the individual soldiers who remained with it after enduring the great hardships in Canada and at Île-aux-Noix; they demonstrated an unshakable devotion to the American cause. The Continental Congress's adoption of the Declaration of Independence added to this commitment by giving the soldiers an ultimate and concrete goal for which to fight. Nineteen-year-old Ezra Blasdell, who served on Lake Champlain that summer, recalled the "great joy among the officers & soldiers" upon hearing the news.

A final element in strengthening the army and Fort Ticonderoga involved possessing a fleet to control Lake Champlain. Allen and Arnold's raids in May 1775 had given the colonists this advantage, and it loomed even larger following the defeat in Canada. The existence of American warships on the lake forced Carleton to construct a fleet to counter these before he could move south, and this took time. Gates appointed Arnold, who had extensive sailing experience, to command this force in July 1776, after its original commander, Jacobus Wynkoop, demonstrated little ability.

Three different types of vessels eventually composed the American fleet. The first type were sailing ships. These included the schooners *Liberty*, *Royal Savage*, and *Revenge*, and the sloop *Enterprise*, all of which the Americans had captured the previous year. They also had the cutter *Lee*, which the soldiers had found partly constructed at Saint-Jean and took with them when they evacuated Canada. These ships were a solid nucleus for a fleet, but they alone would not be enough.

Schuyler also knew the importance of controlling the lake, and he made a concerted effort to strengthen this fleet. As early as April 1776, he sent Hermanus Schuyler, a distant relative, to Skenesborough to develop a shipyard, where the Americans began constructing the second category of warships, gondolas. Similar to oversized bateaux, gondolas were 50-foot-long, flat-bottomed vessels with fixed sails that could only work when the wind blew from astern. Gondola crews could row these vessels, but they lacked speed and maneuverability. Beginning in late July, the Skenesborough shipwrights began building a third type of vessel, row galleys. These highly maneuverable round-bottom vessels were approximately 80 feet long and rigged so as to sail both with and into the wind, in addition to being fitted with oars. They also carried larger, more numerous cannons than the other vessels.

Constructing such a fleet in the wilderness was an enormous logistical undertaking. Arnold often receives credit for this achievement, and he provided much of the force and energy behind it, but others also merit recognition. Both Philip and Hermanus Schuyler played a role, as did Philip's aide-de-camp, Capt. Richard Varick, who coordinated much of the supply effort. Connecticut Brig. Gen. David Waterbury oversaw much of the actual construction at Skenesborough. The Americans initially lacked enough trained shipbuilders, so they brought in highly paid artisans from Pennsylvania and New England. By the end of July, 200 of them worked at Skenesborough, although an outbreak of illness delayed their efforts. To complete the vessels, the shipwrights and carpenters needed large amounts of sawed lumber, iron, ropes, and other items. This included 2,500 oars, which Gates ordered made at Crown Point. Once the builders finished the vessels' hulls, crews rowed them to Ticonderoga, where other workers fitted them with riggings, which created a demand for sails. Still other workers mounted the vessels with cannons. Although the Americans possessed enough of these weapons, they were of inferior quality and weight to those that the British fleet carried. Perhaps most importantly, the ships lacked trained sailors, so Gates drafted into service soldiers from at least four different regiments. At least ten members of the Stockbridge tribe also accompanied the vessels. Despite the obstacles, by October Arnold's fleet consisted of the five sailing vessels, three row galleys—the *Congress*, *Trumbull*, and *Washington*—and eight gondolas. The ships carried ninety-four cannons in total, ranging from 2-pounders to 18-pounders, in addition to numerous swivel guns, small-bored cannons used against boarding parties and against bateaux, canoes, and similar light craft. Arnold ultimately used the *Lee* as a messenger vessel and the *Enterprise* as a hospital ship, because of their small size and limited military capacity.

As the Americans constructed their fleet at the southern end of Lake Champlain, Carleton's troops did the same at Saint-Jean. The British had a distinct advantage in their large number of trained sailors, as well as artillery pieces designed for warships, drawing both from their fleet in the St. Lawrence. The relief force also had brought the pieces of fourteen flat-bottom gunboats that workers could assemble in short order. The rapids on the Richelieu River between Chambly and Saint-Jean, however, posed a major obstacle and slowed the British efforts. The British managed to haul one gondola, the *Loyal Convert*, and 400 bateaux through these rapids but were unable to transport larger vessels this way. Therefore, British sailors disassembled two ships—the *Maria* and *Carleton*—and transported the pieces overland to Saint-Jean, and then reassembled them. The British also built approximately twenty-five gunboats there, including the prefabricated ones, and an enormous seven-sided *radeau*, the *Thunderer*. Rigged with sails, this 91-foot-long floating battery carried two 8-inch howitzers, six 24-pound cannons, and six 12-pound cannons.

In late August, with the British fleet nearing completion, Carleton received intelligence that the pugnacious Arnold intended to attack the British shipyard at Saint-Jean with his fleet. To counter this threat and to ensure he had overwhelming strength, Carleton ordered his shipwrights to disassemble a third vessel, the sloop of war *Inflexible*, and then transport and rebuild it at Saint-Jean. This process took more than a month. The workers did not complete the *Inflexible*, the most powerful ship in the British Lake Champlain squadron, until 3 October. At this point, Carleton's fleet, commanded by Capt. Thomas Pringle, numbered five major vessels and approximately twenty gunboats, carrying at least eighty-five cannons, ranging from 6- to 24-pounders. The combined weight of the British broadside was more than 1,000 pounds compared to 600 for the American fleet.

As it turned out, Arnold had no intention of attacking Saint-Jean, but was doing everything he could to delay the British advance, including planting false information about his intentions. Gates's orders called for the fleet to sail no farther north than just across the Canadian border and not to undertake offensive actions.

Battle of Valcour Island, V. Zveg, ca. 1962 (Naval History and Heritage Command)

Still, by 24 August, Arnold's fleet headed to the north end of Lake Champlain, attempting to keep Carleton on the defensive. This gave his green crews valuable sailing experience and bought time for the American cause. The American row galleys had not yet joined the fleet, and Arnold knew that Ticonderoga lacked enough gunpowder to resist a major British attack, despite Gates and Schuyler's efforts. Additionally, on 9 September, Arnold learned of the Battle of Long Island on 27 August. Although this initial garbled report suggested that Washington had defeated the British, Arnold still wanted to delay Carleton's advance and possible cooperation with Lt. Gen. William Howe's army as long as possible. Sailing on the north end of the lake provided Arnold with the opportunity to select the best location to fight.

By 15 September, the American commander had chosen heavily wooded Valcour Island, near the New York side of the lake, about halfway between Ticonderoga and Saint-Jean. Arnold intended to anchor his fleet behind the south end of the island. Shoals and

Royal Savage, Lt. Enant Calderwood (*Naval History and Heritage Command*)

a narrow channel between the island and the west shore of the lake blocked any British ships from approaching it from the north. Furthermore, the forest would hide Arnold's vessels from the British fleet until it sailed past the island on its east side, forcing Carleton's ships to turn around and head into the wind. This would allow the stationary American ships to engage the British vessels piecemeal, and Arnold's crews would not have to outsail and outmaneuver the British fleet. Arnold took up his station behind Valcour Island on 24 September, and the row galleys arrived by 6 October.

Carleton's fleet sailed from Saint-Jean on 4 October. After fending off an invasion and learning of the Declaration of Independence, Carleton now saw the benefits of deploying Native Americans. Approximately 800 Iroquois, Algonquin, Hurons, and other groups accompanied the vessels in canoes as they made their way south on Lake Champlain, as did hundreds of British soldiers in bateaux. At 1000 on 11 October, propelled by a strong north wind, the British reached Valcour Island with Carleton's five large warships in front, followed by the gunboats, and then the canoe and bateaux. Pringle failed to deploy any scouting vessels, and, just as Arnold had hoped, the British did not see the American ships until they had sailed past him. Pringle ordered the fleet to turn around. Although the maneuverable British gunboats managed to do this, the larger ships struggled against the wind. Arnold, alerted of the British approach by some Stockbridge Mohicans he had stationed on the northern end of the island, had his fifteen ships ready.

To ensure that Pringle and Carleton engaged, Arnold ordered the *Royal Savage* and the three row galleys, the *Congress*, *Trumbull*, and *Washington*, to sail toward the scattered British vessels, firing as they went. After a brief foray, the American ships turned into the wind and made their way back toward their original anchorage. The three row galleys accomplished this, but the *Royal Savage* ran into difficulties. As it attempted to sail north, British fire shredded its rigging, and a shot hit one of its masts. The vessel ran aground on the southern edge of Valcour Island. Several British gunboats then pounded the ship, but the crew escaped.

Deployed in a crescent, Arnold's vessels then traded fire with the gunboats, which stayed about 700 yards away. Pascal DeAngelis, the 12-year-old stepson of the *Trumbull*'s captain, wrote that "the Enemy Fleet attaced ours with Great fury and we Returned the fire with as Great Sperit and Viger." The larger British vessels were generally beyond effective range and did not actively engage, with two exceptions. The *Loyal Convert* managed to approach Valcour Island, and a boarding party of twenty rowed to the *Royal Savage* and turned its guns on the Americans. This assault did not last long. The wind again pushed the *Loyal Convert* away from the ship, and American return fire killed or wounded half of the boarding party, which then abandoned the grounded *Royal Savage*. The *Carleton* also became engaged heavily. Battling against the wind, the 12-gun schooner sailed through the British gunboats and dropped anchor about 350 yards from Arnold's line. It then opened a powerful point-blank barrage, which the Americans responded to in kind, concentrating their fire on the ship. While the two fleets battled, British soldiers and Native Americans landed on the island and the adjacent shore and opened fire on Arnold's ships. This also produced a reaction as DeAngelis remembered. "[T]he Regulars and Indians fired with small armes . . . att the Galley Washington who soon put them in Silence by a Few Cannester Shott."

The slugging match continued for six hours until darkness fell, and Arnold withdrew his fleet several hundred yards to assess the situation. In addition to losing the *Royal Savage*, which the British burned, the gondola *Philadelphia* sustained heavy damage and sank that evening. British cannonballs had repeatedly hit the *Congress* and *Washington*, along with many of the gondolas, and had killed or wounded approximately sixty American sailors. Arnold's vessels were also running low on ammunition. On the British side, the *Carleton* had received heavy punishment which left its captain wounded, and a gunboat manned by Hessians sank after its magazine exploded.

Arnold realized that he could not remain at Valcour Island and decided to escape south to Crown Point. Carleton's gunboats had withdrawn to replenish their ammunition, leaving an unguarded route along the New York shore. The American vessels silently rowed away in single file in the darkness, and, after several hours, left the British fleet behind. The following morning, the British were shocked to find Arnold gone. When scouting vessels saw no signs of the Americans to the north, Carleton ordered his ships to sail south, but contrary winds slowed their pursuit. Meanwhile, Arnold and his battered fleet briefly anchored at Schuyler Island, where they scuttled or sank three of the damaged gondolas. They then proceeded south, with the *Congress*, Arnold's flagship, and the *Washington*, acting as the rear guard. Strong winds, however, prevented the American vessels—especially the ungainly gondolas—from making much progress.

On 13 October, the wind shifted to the north, and Carleton's fleet rapidly bore down upon the American vessels, with the *Inflexible*, *Maria*, and repaired *Carleton* in the lead. They caught Arnold's ships near Split Rock and immediately opened fire, prompting the *Washington* to quickly surrender. Arnold fought a running battle for several hours covering 9 miles with the *Congress*

Battle of Lake Champlain (Naval History and Heritage Command)

and four gondolas. Finally, he ordered the five vessels to land on the eastern shore of the lake, where their crews set them afire, and they returned to Ticonderoga by foot the next day. Nineteen-year-

Ernest Haas. *Cannon Exploding on the Gunboat New York off Valcour Island*. Acrylic on Panel. 2002.024.001 (*Lake Champlain Maritime Museum Collection*)

old Clement Tuttle wrote, "the American fleet was dispersed and defeated, and that the Congress Galley was stranded, and the crew obliged to swim ashore under the fire of the British fleet; That after gaining the shore, . . . he lay in the woods in the ensuing night." That evening the few remaining vessels of Arnold's fleet arrived back at Ticonderoga.

The news of the destruction of the fleet prompted the Americans to redouble their efforts to strengthen Ticonderoga and adjacent Mount Independence by building additional redoubts and other fortifications. With the British now controlling the lake, Gates ordered the construction of a boom between the two forts to prevent warships from forcing their way into the upper end of the lake and Skenesborough. The Americans began to build this log-and-chain barrier on 17 October and completed it on the 25th. The arrival of additional shipments of gunpowder and at least 800 militiamen who turned out to meet the British threat further bolstered the American defenses. By 9 November, Gates reported his strength at 8,900 officers and enlisted men, but by this point, the British threat was gone.

On 13 October, the British fleet arrived at Crown Point, which a small American advance guard quickly abandoned. Over the next several days, Carleton's troops landed there as he considered his next move. It was late in the season, and he lacked the equipment for a lengthy siege of Ticonderoga. Furthermore, blustery winds

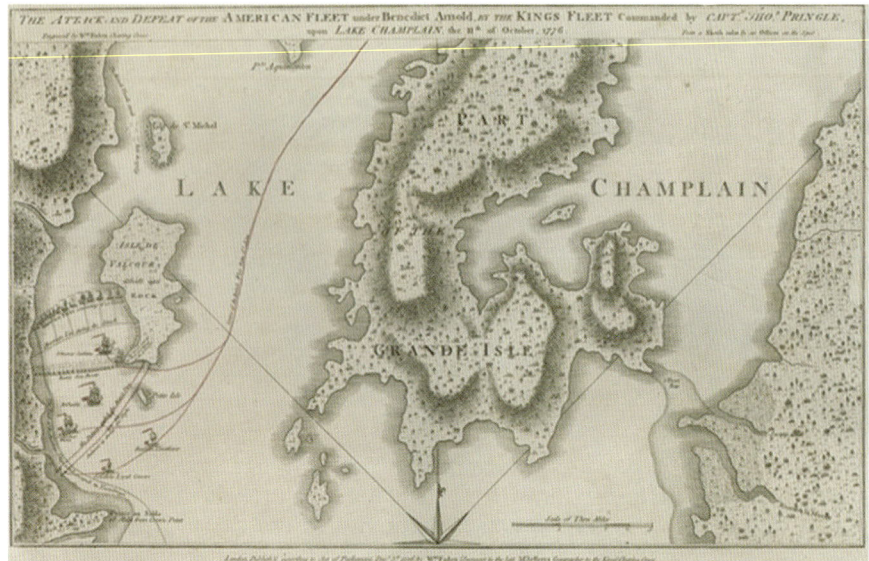

Detail of "The attack and defeat of the American fleet under Benedict Arnold, by the Kings fleet commanded by Capt. Thos. Pringle, upon Lake Champlain, the 11th of October, 1776" by William Faden (*Boston Public Library*)

prevented his sailing ships from approaching the fort. Finally, on 28 October, after a two week pause, two groups of British gunboats, one of which carried the British general, neared Ticonderoga. As they did so, large numbers of American soldiers appeared behind strong fortifications that lined both sides of Lake Champlain. A cannon then opened fire and hit one of the gunboats, damaging the craft and inflicting casualties. The British vessels returned to Crown Point. Three days after this brief reconnaissance, Carleton issued a general order which read in part, "the severity of the approaching season render[s] it impossible to pursue the rebels any further this year without endangering the health of the troops." Many British officers, most notably Burgoyne, disagreed with this decision, believing that Carleton was missing an important opportunity to take Ticonderoga and deal the American rebellion a serious blow. On 2 November the British boarded their vessels and sailed for Saint-Jean.

Gates and Schuyler reallocated their forces after they realized that the British had withdrawn to Canada. They dismissed the militia and those regiments whose enlistment had expired, and designated troops to spend the winter at Ticonderoga. Most significantly, Gates took several regiments south to reinforce George Washington's Army, which was retreating toward Pennsylvania before William Howe's forces. These troops arrived near the Delaware River on 21 December, days before the Battles of Trenton and Princeton. With the British back in Saint-Jean and the Americans holding Ticonderoga, the Canadian Campaign had ended.

CONCLUSION AND ANALYSIS

The Continental Army failed to conquer Canada and prompt its inhabitants to unite with the Americans against Britain for several interrelated reasons. First, and most importantly, the colonies and their congress, which had not yet even declared independence, lacked the organization and resources to maintain a large military operation in Canada, especially during the winter. The Continental Congress was still relatively new and finding its way, and was in essence a committee coordinating the efforts of thirteen separate colonies. As such, its authority was limited and relied on consensus, which often came slowly. Trying to provide for Washington's Army besieging Boston, negotiating with Britain, dealing with the disparate concerns of the colonies, raising funds, and addressing a host of other issues, proved to be too much for this relatively weak system of governance. In part because of the limitations of the Continental Congress and in part because of the paucity of manufacturing capability, chronic shortages of weapons, gunpowder, clothing, provisions, and medicine hindered American military operations throughout the campaign. The lack of hard money to pay for supplies exacerbated these problems and alienated the civilian population.

These issues led to another cause of the American failure, the lack of widespread Canadian support. Both the First and Second Continental Congress attempted to convince the Canadians that they shared a common cause in opposing British tyranny. The Americans then received a steady stream of intelligence suggesting that both Old and New Subjects would welcome an invasion. In the end, this information was inaccurate. Some Canadians assisted the invaders with provisions and intelligence either for money or because they supported their cause. In other cases, some took up arms with them as a way of opposing the Quebec Act or defying their seigneurs and the Catholic church. Most Canadians, however, did not go over to the American side. Catholic seigneurs and habitants had little in common with the English-speaking Protestant invaders. They also wanted additional evidence that the Americans could drive the British from the colony permanently. Until this happened, many Canadians willingly sat on the sidelines as observers in a war that was not of their making. The Continental Army's actions, especially once it occupied Montréal and the areas outside Québec City, further undercut Canadian support. The locals disliked and distrusted paper Continental currency, and they greatly resented hungry soldiers requisitioning their food. Relations soured further as the American military situation in Canada deteriorated in the spring of 1776.

Leadership, which proved wanting at all levels, was another cause of the American failure. Despite repeated requests from Schuyler and Montgomery, Congress neglected to send a delegation to Canada to handle administrative and diplomatic affairs until the spring of 1776. By this time, the American position there largely had collapsed, and the committee could do little to reverse this trend. Military leadership proved inconsistent. Montgomery and Arnold conducted their operations in an exemplary manner overcoming numerous obstacles, and they besieged Québec City but ultimately could not force its surrender. They also both demonstrated great personal courage and won their soldiers' confidence, but this show of valor had a high price. Montgomery, the ranking officer in Canada, died at the head of his troops while storming Québec, and Arnold received a serious wound in the same assault. The generals who took their places were less effective. Elderly David Wooster alienated many Canadians and did not travel to Québec City until three months after the failed assault. John Thomas had little opportunity to demonstrate his talents before he died of smallpox, which thrust the newly arrived John Sullivan into command. By this point, thousands of British reinforcements had landed in Canada, much of the civilian population had turned on the Americans, and disease and defeat had demoralized the army. Both Gates and Schuyler performed admirably in rebuilding and restoring the Northern Army between July and October 1776, an achievement which one historian hails as "one of the single most impressive accomplishments in American military history." Although their efforts saved Ticonderoga and possibly the American cause, this was a defensive operation and did not help conquer Canada.

Disease, most notably smallpox, was yet another cause of the American defeat in Canada. From the time of its first appearance in December through the following summer, smallpox ravaged Continental forces, especially the arriving troops. As the deadly epidemic spread, many soldiers resorted to inoculations, both supervised and unsupervised, which further transmitted the disease. The losses caused by sickness sapped regiments of their strength and destroyed the command structure, which created additional difficulties. The Continental Army's lack of resources, the limited Canadian support for their actions, indifferent leadership, and disease all combined to doom the American effort to seize Canada.

Despite these considerations, the Canadian invasion was not a complete failure. It bought the Americans valuable time, during which they strengthened their resolve and further prepared for war. Montgomery's and Arnold's efforts prevented any British attack on the New York and New England frontier in 1775. This bulwark to the north allowed Congress and Washington to focus their efforts on combating General Thomas Gage's forces in Boston. Carleton then spent most of 1776 driving the Americans from Canada and building a fleet to challenge them on Lake Champlain. Although he succeeded in his efforts, this mission consumed the entire campaign season, and he was unable to cooperate with Howe's campaign on the Hudson River. Had he done so, perhaps the American rebellion would have ended that fall. Instead, the British would have to wait until 1777 to try to unite their forces in Canada with those coming from New York City. The invasion similarly complicated Britain's war plans, by forcing it to deploy more than 12,000 soldiers and other resources to Canada, rendering them unavailable for other areas such as New York City or New England. Britain also kept large numbers of troops in Canada for the remainder of the war to deter future American incursions.

The Canadian invasion provided many American officers and soldiers valuable military experience. Twelve future Continental Army generals served in Canada, including Daniel Morgan, John Stark, and Anthony Wayne. These officers made important contributions later in the war at such engagements as Cowpens, Bennington, and Yorktown. The same is true for dozens of field officers, such as Henry Dearborn, a veteran of Arnold's march to Québec, and leader of light infantry at Saratoga. Marinus Willett and Peter Gansevoort, who helped repel the British attack on the Mohawk Valley in 1777, served with Montgomery in Canada. Hundreds of enlisted men had similar experiences. One study of 733 soldiers associated with the Battle of Bennington found that at least 73 served in Canada in 1775 or 1776. Despite the hardships they endured at Saint-Jean, Québec City, and Île-aux-Noix, these veteran troops remained committed to American independence and continued to serve.

Finally, the Canadian Campaign helped convince Congress of the importance of long-term enlistments. Montgomery and Arnold rushed their assault on Québec because of expiring short-term enlistments, much as George Washington would do a year later at Trenton when facing a similar circumstance. The congressional committee that traveled to Canada in the spring of 1776 came to this conclusion, as did others. That autumn, Congress voted to enlarge the Continental Army and offer bounties for soldiers who enlisted for the duration of the war. When John Hancock, the president of the Continental Congress, informed Washington of this decision he cited Montgomery's "untimely Death" as "striking proof of the Danger and Impropriety of sending troops into the Field under any Restrictions as to the Time of their Service."

In the end, it remains debatable as to whether the Americans could have permanently held Canada, even if Montgomery and Arnold had captured Québec City. The British reinforcements that arrived in May 1776 possessed overwhelming strength, and the Canadian people never wholeheartedly embraced the American position by sending delegates to the Continental Congress. Perhaps the entire invasion and the ideas behind it were a lost cause from the start. Still, the Canadian invasion bought the American revolutionaries critical time to strengthen their cause, declare independence, and gain valuable experience for the long war ahead.

 # APPENDIX

"Order, Regularity, & Discipline": Waging War in the Eighteenth Century

by Joseph A. Seymour

By 1775, armies in Europe and North America had developed into complex forces organized around the infantry regiment. Artillery provided fire support. Mounted units performed reconnaissance, screened attacks and retreats, and added shock. Engineers and pioneers built and demolished fortifications and other works. Artificers repaired and maintained weapons and ordnance. Surgeons treated the sick and wounded. Civilian commissaries made, procured, and transported supplies and rations. All of them supported the foot soldiers, who usually dominated the battlefield.

Composition

The Continental Army and state militia generally organized their infantry regiments using the British model, with a colonel in command, aided by a lieutenant colonel, major, and regimental staff. A regiment had ten companies, including one light and one grenadier company. The light company consisted of the best shots, the cleverest, and the most agile in the regiment. These soldiers specialized in screening, skirmishing, patrolling, and scouting. Congress dispensed early on with the grenadier company, with its brawny shock troops who often formed the vanguard of assaults, and usually authorized nine companies. Each company carried equipment and additional ammunition in one or two wagons. When the situation called for the infantry to operate away from its baggage train, soldiers placed extra ammunition and essential items in their knapsacks. Most companies had a few women on their rolls. Although not officially in the army, they could draw rations, and sometimes pay, by performing various essential duties, including nursing the sick and wounded and laundering the soldiers' clothing. Captains and lieutenants directed the maneuver and fire of the platoons in their companies. Sergeants and corporals maintained unit cohesion in battle, assisted officers, and enforced discipline in the sections under their charge. Drummers, who ranked between corporals and sergeants, communicated orders in camp and battle.

Equipment

A soldier's basic fighting equipment was known as a stand of arms, which commonly consisted of a musket; a bayonet; a cartridge box of wood, leather, or tin containing between twenty-three and twenty-nine paper cartridges; and cleaning tools. A standard firearm of the period was the British Land Pattern musket. It fired a powerful load consisting of a 1-ounce lead ball propelled by nearly a half ounce of gunpowder. Its oversized barrel of about 0.76- to 0.80-inch diameter made it easier to load. A ball fired from a musket of this type could reach massed troops out to 300 yards. At 100 yards, it was accurate enough to hit an individual and powerful enough to penetrate a two-inch elm plank. Continental, state, and militia forces augmented existing musket stores with locally made copies of the Land Pattern and imported French, German, Dutch, and Spanish arms of similar bore sizes and ballistics. Soldiers also shouldered sporting (nonmilitary issue) arms of different calibers, sometimes retrofitted to mount bayonets. The lack of serviceable arms slowed augmentation and the integration of reinforcements. Furthermore, companies equipped with a mix of arms could not easily sustain fire, let alone mount effective bayonet assaults.

Both armies also issued rifles to light troops or recruited experienced riflemen who brought their own. The rifles usually followed two patterns: the short-barreled, large-bore Germanic or *Jäger* (hunter) rifle, and the long-barreled, small-bore Pennsylvania rifle. Less powerful than muskets, both were accurate to about 300 yards and took about one minute to load. Neither could mount a bayonet. In 1777, British Maj. Patrick Ferguson fielded an innovative breech-loading rifle that mounted a bayonet, but it saw limited service.

Tactics

The musket's capabilities shaped tactics. A trained soldier could fire three rounds per minute. After twenty-five shots, the piece became too hot to handle, and the accumulation of residual gunpowder (known as powder-fouling) required cleaning and slowed reloading. Regiments formed in line at close order, presenting a continuous front of muskets and bayonets to concentrate their fire and mass to maximum effect. Close ranks also enabled company commanders to keep their troops together and thus better control them. The soldiers easily could hear orders communicated by drumbeat and could support each other using linear tactics described in tactical publications such as the *Manual Exercise, As Ordered by His Majesty in 1764*. In 1778, the Continental Army introduced a system spelled out in the *Regulations for the Order and Discipline of the Troops of the United States*, nicknamed the Blue Book. Well-drilled companies could execute a variety of maneuvers to bring their firepower or bayonets to bear, unleashing simultaneous volleys with devastating effect, or firing alternately by platoon to sustain a running fire. Infantry usually closed to the optimal range of 40 yards for a killing volley before a bayonet assault. While battalions also could extend their intervals to optimize individual fire, volume rather than accuracy usually decided a battle's outcome.

Artillery on both sides organized as separate regiments and battalions but fought as detachments as needed. With a range of several hundred yards, 3-, 4-, and 6-pounder guns supported battalions in battle. With their slightly longer range, 8- and 12-pounders supported brigades, while larger guns with greater range operated from fortifications. Mortars fired exploding shells in a high arc to get over walls or other obstacles. Howitzers fired shells either directly at troops or in an arc. Artillerists and wagon teams were valuable assets. Commanders therefore often ordered crews that were about to be overrun by the enemy to disable their guns with spikes and mallets and abandon the weapons to save themselves and their teams.

Both forces also employed light dragoons, a type of mounted infantry. The scarcity of large horse breeds in America, the cost of transporting such mounts, and the uneven topography challenged the use of cavalry. Organized as regiments or separate troops, dragoons fought both mounted and dismounted and were armed with sabers, carbines, and, occasionally, pistols. Depending on time and terrain, both armies frequently detached light infantry, riflemen, artillery, and dragoons into separate battalions or combined them into corps or legions.

Fortifications

European and colonial governments constructed dozens of forts before and during the war to defend important cities, towns, and key points. Field fortifications included fort-like redoubts, arrow-shaped flèches, and crescent-shaped lunettes. These structures were built of large wicker cylinders, called gabions, which were filled with soil or rubble, and then reinforced by bundles of sticks called fascines, covered with soil and sod, and surrounded by moats. As time permitted, soldiers erected palisades (walls of vertical wooden stakes), placed fraises (sharpened stakes) at a slant on the inner surface of the moat, and laid an abatis (a network of felled trees with sharpened branches) to slow infantry assaults. For a portable obstacle, artificers would use a cheval-de-frise, which typically consisted of sharpened stakes projecting from a log or beam. To fortify harbor defenses and block rivers, engineers employed log booms connected with heavy chains and created the naval version of a cheval-de-frise by constructing rock-filled timber boxes bearing sharpened logs.

Technology dictated tactics, which in turn influenced formations. The contending forces frequently deviated from the standards prescribed by regulations or government allocations as they dealt with issues of personnel, materiel, and authority. Necessity and mission spurred the evolution of regulations, tactics, and equipment during the war. That was particularly the case for the new army of the United States. As the war progressed, American soldiers attained a high level of proficiency that earned the confidence of those they served and the respect of both allies and enemies.

> "The Course of human Affairs forbids an Expectation, that Troops formed under such Circumstances, should at once posses the Order, Regularity & Discipline of Veterans—Whatever Deficiencies there may be, will I doubt not, soon be made up by the Activity & Zeal of the Officers, and the Docility & Obedience of the Men. These Quali[ties,] united with their native Bravery, & Spirit will afford a happy Presage of Success, & put a final Period to those Distresses which now overwhelm this once happy Country."
>
> —George Washington, in an address to the Massachusetts Provincial Congress, 4 July 1775

 # BIBLIOGRAPHIC NOTE

This monograph is based largely on secondary sources. Several works regarding the campaign and its main players are listed below. A primary source consulted was the Revolutionary War Pension and Bounty Land Warrant Application Files at the National Archives, Washington, D.C. These files were accessed via Fold3.com, an online repository of historical military records.

Anderson, Mark R. *The Battle for the Fourteenth Colony: America's War of Liberation in Canada, 1774–1776.* Hanover, NH: University Press of New England, 2013.

Bellico, Russell P. *Sails and Steam in the Mountains: A Maritime and Military History of Lake George and Lake Champlain*, rev. ed. Fleischmanns, NY: Purple Mountain Press, 2001.

Cubbison, Douglas R. *The American Northern Theater Army in 1776: The Ruin and Reconstruction of the Continental Force.* Jefferson, NC: McFarland & Co., 2010.

Desjardin, Thomas A. *Through a Howling Wilderness: Benedict Arnold's March to Quebec, 1775.* New York: St. Martin's Press, 2006.

Gabriel, Michael P. *Major General Richard Montgomery: The Making of an American Hero.* Madison, NJ: Fairleigh Dickinson University Press, 2002.

Lefkowitz, Arthur S. *Benedict Arnold's Army: The 1775 American Invasion of Canada during the Revolutionary War.* New York: Savas Beatie, 2008.

Martin, James Kirby. "The Battle of Valcour Island." In *Great American Naval Battles*, ed. Jack Sweetman. Annapolis, MD: Naval Institute Press, 1998.

Morrissey, Brendan. *Quebec 1775: The American Invasion of Canada*. Botley, UK: Osprey Publishing, 2003.

Nelson, James L. *Benedict Arnold's Navy: The Ragtag Fleet that Lost the Battle of Lake Champlain but Won the American Revolution*. Camden, ME: McGraw Hill, 2006.

Stanley, George F. G. *Canada Invaded, 1775–1776*. Toronto: Samuel Stevens Hakkert, 1977.

Series Sources

The following sources were used to prepare the entire "U.S. Army Campaigns of the Revolutionary War" series of monographs and are recommended for further reading:

Blackmore, David. *Destructive and Formidable: British Infantry Firepower, 1642–1765*. London: Frontline Books, 2014.

Mayer, Holly A. *Belonging to the Army: Camp Followers and Community during the American Revolution*. Columbia: University of South Carolina Press, 1996.

Peterson, Harold L. *Forts in America*. New York: Charles Scribner's Sons, 1964.

———. *Round Shot and Rammers*. Harrisburg, PA: Stackpole Books, 1969.

Risch, Erna. *Supplying Washington's Army*. Washington, DC: U.S. Army Center of Military History, 1981.

Rothenberg, Gunther. *The Art of Warfare in the Age of Napoleon*. Bloomington: University of Indiana Press, 1980.

Spring, Matthew H. *With Zeal and Bayonets Only: The British Army on Campaign in North America, 1775–1783*. Norman: University of Oklahoma Press, 2008.

Wright, Robert K., Jr. *The Continental Army*. Washington, DC U.S. Army Center of Military History, 2006 (revision forthcoming).

 # THE AUTHOR

Michael P. Gabriel is chair of the Department of History at Kutztown University of Pennsylvania. He earned his master's and doctorate at Saint Bonaventure and Penn State Universities, respectively. He is the author of *Major General Richard Montgomery: The Making of an American Hero* (Fairleigh Dickinson University Press, 2002) and *The Battle of Bennington: Soldiers and Civilians* (History Press, 2012). He is the editor of *Quebec During the American Invasion, 1775–1776: The Journal of François Baby, Gabriel Taschereau, and Jenkin Williams* (Michigan State University Press, 2005) and *Physician Soldier: The South Pacific Letters of Captain Fred Gabriel from the 39th Station Hospital* (Texas A&M University Press, 2020).

ACKNOWLEDGMENT

The U.S. Army Center of Military History gratefully acknowledges the Lake Champlain Maritime Museum for the free use of *Cannon Exploding Aboard Gunboat New York, October 17, 1776* by Ernie Haas.